EARTHLY KNOWLEDGE
AND HEAVENLY WISDOM

EARTHLY KNOWLEDGE AND HEAVENLY WISDOM

*Nine Lectures held in Dornach
between February 2 and February 18, 1923*

RUDOLF STEINER

Translated by Sabine H. Seiler

ANTHROPOSOPHIC PRESS

This book is a translation of *Erdenwissen und Himmelserkenntnis* (volume 221 in the Collected Works), published by Rudolf Steiner Verlag, Dornach, Switzerland, 1981.

The publishers would like to acknowledge the work of Pauline Wehrle, who made an earlier translation of this volume that was a helpful basis for this current version.

All Bible quotations in this book are taken from *The New Oxford Annotated Bible*, Revised Standard Version.

Published in the United States by Anthroposophic Press, R.R. 4, Box 94 A1, Hudson, New York 12534.

Copyright © 1991 by Anthroposophic Press, Inc.

Library of Congress Cataloging-in-Publication Data

Steiner, Rudolf, 1861–1925.
   [Erdenwissen und Himmelserkenntnis. English]
   Earthly knowledge and heavenly wisdom : nine lectures held in Dornach between February 2 and February 18, 1923 / Rudolf Steiner : translated by Sabine H. Seiler.
    Translation of: Erdenwissen und Himmelserkenntnis.
    Includes bibliographical references.
    ISBN 0-88010-295-0 — ISBN 0-88010-294-2 (pbk.)
    1. Anthroposophy. I. Seiler, Sabine H. II. Title.
BP595.S894E7313   1990
299′.935—dc20   90-21616
                                                  CIP

Printed in the United States of America

CONTENTS

LECTURE ONE
February 2, 1923
Self-Knowledge and Experiencing the Christ in
Oneself
1

LECTURE TWO
February 3, 1923
The Human Being in Waking and in Sleeping
Part I
16

LECTURE THREE
February 4, 1923
The Human Being in Waking and in Sleeping
Part II
33

LECTURE FOUR
February 9, 1923
Earthly Learning and Heavenly Wisdom: Human
Beings as Citizens of the Universe and Hermits
on the Earth
Part I
41

LECTURE FIVE
February 10, 1923
Earthly Learning and Heavenly Wisdom: Human
Beings as Citizens of the Universe and Hermits
on the Earth
Part II

54

LECTURE SIX
February 11, 1923
The Invisible Human Being Within Us

69

BLACKBOARD ILLUSTRATIONS

87

LECTURE SEVEN
February 16, 1923
Moral Impulses and their Physical
Manifestations: Taking Up a Spiritual Path
Part I

90

LECTURE EIGHT
February 17, 1923
Moral Impulses and Their Physical
Manifestations: Taking Up a Spiritual Path
Part II

105

LECTURE NINE
February 18, 1923
Moral Impulses and Their Physical
Manifestations: Taking Up a Spiritual Path
Part III

120

Notes

138

Publisher's Note

147

EARTHLY KNOWLEDGE
AND HEAVENLY WISDOM

February 2, 1923

SELF-KNOWLEDGE AND EXPERIENCING THE CHRIST IN ONESELF

ANIMALS PARTICIPATE in a certain way in an annual cycle: Butterflies and other insects are in their chrysalis stage in one season, hatch in another, and lay their eggs in still another. We can see a relationship between the changes in nature and the life cycle of insects; they adapt their lives to their natural environment. Similarly, in previous ages of earth evolution, human communities participated more or less instinctively in the life of outer nature. However, as human evolution advanced, the instincts that enabled people to participate in their immediate natural environment largely disappeared. In our more advanced stage we no longer find this kind of outer harmony between the natural surroundings and the individual human being. This is connected with our evolution, which constitutes our history and forms a unified whole extending over the long epochs of the earth's planetary evolution.

Let us look more closely at the lower animals, such as insects, because things are clearer and simpler there. These animals live out their lives in a relatively short period of time, for example, in a year. After that, the same processes are repeated in the following generations. In human evolution, there is a similar regular pattern for longer periods. For instance, we have found that, in ancient times, people had a kind of instinctive clairvoyance, a picture consciousness. This then faded in the middle period of human evolution with the transition from the ancient picture consciousness to the modern intellectual and conceptual consciousness. Our current historical period, which began with the first third of the fifteenth century, was a period of development of the consciousness soul; it was the age when humanity entered into intellectual thinking in the strict sense, and this led us for the first time to completely free self-awareness.

When we consider a long period of time from this perspective, we find a certain overall regularity in the whole of human evolution. This regularity is analogous to what we find in an insect's life in the course of a year.

Now, in ancient times, people still enjoyed a certain instinctive participation in the natural cycles of their environment. But these instincts have largely declined, and now conscious inner life must take the place of the old instinctive life. It must guide us, for if we left our lives completely to chance, without any inner guidelines or rules, and without ever deciding on a direction for our entire being—in other words, if we never found our inner bearings, but left our life here on earth entirely under the sway of chance— then, even though our soul life is more developed than that of animals, we would sink below the animal level.

For example, insects have a certain orientation in their life in spring, summer, fall, and winter. They are not dominated by the accidents of the process of becoming, but are integrated into the world through the regularity of the sequence of their various life phases. We left behind the ancient instinctive participation in nature, which, even though it was instinctive, was still more a matter of soul than that of the animals. In its place, we have taken on a newer, more conscious form of participation. However, despite our higher soul– and thought-life, with the decline of our instincts we have entered a more chaotic existence and have thereby sunk in a certain way below the animal level.

No matter how much we stress our superiority to the animal kingdom and the progress we have made in our evolution, we have to admit that we have lost our inner sense of direction for our lives. As members of the human race, we have to find this inner sense of direction in the awareness that we belong to this or that century, which, in turn, has a special place in the total evolution of our planet, just as the month of September has a special place in the course of the year. In other words, we have to become aware of how our soul life will enter into our particular historical epoch.

This is something we still have to work on by entering more and more deeply into the development of the consciousness soul. We have to be conscious that we live in this or that epoch and are not fully human if we leave our life to chance, or karma, which has placed us into our earthly existence at birth. We are fully human, in the true sense of the word, only if we take into account what the historical evolution of humanity demands of our soul life in the epoch in which we live. Animals live in accordance with the course of the year. Human beings, on the other hand, have to learn to live in accordance with a historical epoch.

We have said that the Mystery of Golgotha is the most important event in the history of the earth, and we have often talked about what it means to have lived before the

Mystery of Golgotha or at a certain time after it. Indeed, the Mystery of Golgotha is the pivotal point in history, and we can calculate forward and backward in time from this supreme historical event. However, to calculate time properly on this basis, we have to know, in each historical epoch, the task of our soul in that period.

What is usually called history these days cannot help us develop such an awareness for any given epoch. A mere account of how the Persian, Babylonian, Egyptian, Greek, or Roman culture developed does not tell us anything about how to integrate ourselves harmoniously into the historical development of our planet—the way animals are integrated into the course of the year.

We have already studied various historical epochs to develop an idea of what we need to bring to life in our soul in our era. Life is rich and varied, and if we want to understand the reality of human life on earth fully, we must look at it again and again from different points of view. Today, I would like to discuss an aspect of human life that can show us the particular nature of our soul life in our present age.

In very ancient times of human evolution, we find scattered throughout the various inhabited regions of the earth what we have come to know as the Mysteries. The human communities living then developed under the influence of these Mysteries not only in their outer lives, but also psychically and culturally. Depending on their level of maturity, some individuals were taken into the Mysteries and went through a development that brought them to a certain stage of knowing, feeling, and willing. As bearers of such higher faculties, these individuals then rejoined their communities and gave others guidelines for solving life's problems, for inner strength and invigoration of their souls, and for their outer willing and doing. Therefore, we can best study these guidelines for ancient epochs when we look at how they were taught by those who had experienced the Mysteries.

The pupils of the Mysteries had to get to know their surroundings, most importantly the beings in the so-called three kingdoms of nature. The teaching was similar to what we have today, except, as you know, the approach was not as abstract and intellectual as ours. Nowadays, children learn already in first grade to understand the three kingdoms of nature through all kinds of concepts and representations. We come to know the mineral, plant, and animal kingdoms through concepts and ideas, and then try to understand ourselves and our lives. The concepts of the pupils in those ancient Mysteries were not acquired or arrived at in their inner soul-life through logic, observation, and so on, as ours are. Instead, they had to undergo a soul development that enabled them to get a clear picture of the mineral, plant, and animal kingdoms. Thus, people then did not have the abstract concepts we have now; they had images or pictures that would probably seem extravagant and weird to modern intellectual people. They knew through direct experience that what they learned from these images, what they experienced in them, told them something about what was in the minerals, plants, and animals themselves—something that grew in them, manifested and unfolded in them—and they learned from these images.

People in ancient times saw something true to reality where people now see only strange and fantastic myths. In ancient times, people knew that when they looked at an animal in the physical, sensory world, it had a clearly defined outline. However, they were not interested in such definite outlines; rather, they wanted to understand the life that moved everywhere in a flowing stream. They felt this was not possible in sharply defined pictures or concepts but only in liquid, changing, metamorphosing images. This is how things were presented to them in the Mysteries.

However, when the pupils had to advance to self-knowledge on the basis of this Mystery wisdom, they went through a significant crisis in their souls. They had received images of the mineral, plant, and animal realms in the form appropriate to their time. With their dreamlike consciousness, they could also look into the interior of the kingdoms of nature. However, when they received directions from the Mysteries to "know themselves"—which were similar to those given in later times—they had to advance from imaginative knowledge of nature to self-knowledge, they had to go through a crisis in their souls.

Now let me describe this inner crisis. People had filled their soul life by looking at the being of the mineral kingdom spread out before them; they had within themselves the effects of mineral-physical processes. They also had within themselves images of the manifold, interwoven life of plants and animals. They could integrate all three into one mineral-plant-animal world. Then, on the basis of this, they could look inside themselves, and there they found an inner picture of the mineral, plant, and animal kingdoms as well as an inner picture of their working together.

When these people then began carrying out the command, "Know yourself," they were suddenly stopped short by the realization that although they had a manifold picture-world of what lives on the earth apart from human beings—a picture-world rich in forms and colors, inwardly sounding, even musical—yet, this manifold, constantly changing world of many forms and shimmering, radiant, glittering colors and sounds of music was of no help to them in trying to know themselves. They tried to understand themselves in a similar pictorial way, but were unable to do so. True, they could arrive at images of the human being, but they knew from the way they experienced these pictures that they did not represent the true human being. People's experience of these images was different from what they experienced when they felt their own human dignity. They realized the images did not truly represent these feelings.

This crisis of helplessness in achieving self-knowledge led to another experience; that is, people developed a certain fundamental conviction or philosophy of life we can find at the basis of all ancient civilizations. This conviction is the realization of truly enlightened people that here on earth, where minerals, plants, and animals fulfill their intended purpose and reveal their true being in the pictures people have of them, human beings do not reveal their true being.

The philosophy of life fundamental to all ancient civilizations was that human beings do not belong to the earth in the same way as the creatures of the other kingdoms of nature. The real home of our true essence is not on earth but elsewhere, in the supersensible world. This conviction was not unfounded; people arrived at it through a crisis in their soul lives after they had learned everything about nonhuman life on earth that was appropriate for their times. In fact, this inner crisis could be resolved only because people in ancient times were still able to look at pre-earthly life and also at post-earthly life, at life after death.

In a way, every person with functional instincts was aware of a pre-earthly life, which was present throughout earthly life as a pre-earthly memory. On the basis of this pre-earthly life, people then gained knowledge about life after death in the way I described in the so-called French Course.[1] Based on their ancient faculties, people knew that only after death would they be able to see not only the

essence of nature but also their own essence. In those ancient times, people had only the above-mentioned picture
consciousness in the life between birth and death, but not
yet an intellectual consciousness like ours. They developed
this intellectual consciousness only after death, and then
they retained it.

This is the strange thing about the progress of human
evolution: in ancient times, people developed intellectual
consciousness only after they had died, at the time when
we nowadays review our life in images, that is, during the
first three days after death. During life on earth, those ancient people had a dreamlike picture-consciousness, while
we have our intellectual consciousness. They grew only
gradually into the intellectual life after death when they
were liberated from their bodies. This intellectual life could
then give them freedom. In ancient times, people became
free and intellectual beings only after death.

After the candidates of the Mysteries were initiated into
these truths, they could be taught—based on the knowledge
about the human being available at that time—that in this
earthly life their picture consciousness could teach them
only about the nonhuman world. If they looked at themselves to try to gain self-knowledge, they would fail because
they could not perceive themselves in their full human dignity. They had to understand that they would be truly human only after they had passed through the gate of death.
Then they would have pure thinking, which would help
them become free beings.

Interestingly enough, we have the type of consciousness
people in ancient times had only after death—in a sense,
this consciousness moved in the opposite direction to human life, namely, from life after death to the one on earth.
Our advances in evolution, particularly our achievements

since the first third of the fifteenth century, have shifted from our life after death into our earthly life. In other words, the true human essence, which the pupils of the Mysteries could only find in the supersensible life after death, has entered into our earthly life.

A true supersensible stream has entered our life on earth, because it did not move with us from "before" death to "after" death, but in the opposite direction. We have been blessed with something supersensible, and consequently we have taken on the task to become worthy of this supersensible element in our sensory existence. In short, we must gain our inner freedom and acknowledge the supersensible consciously as part of the development of our consciousness soul.

It is indeed true that even though in earlier times people were challenged to know themselves, the answer they found was that self-knowledge is impossible during life on earth because the true human essence does not fully unfold in this life. They had to realize that they were not truly human beings until they entered the supersensible world after death.

At the time of the Mystery of Golgotha, and even in later centuries, people called the human being living on earth "the natural man," following the ancient Mystery wisdom. They believed "the natural man" was not truly and fully human and did not bear the true human essence within himself. They differentiated between this natural human being and the pneumatic or spiritual human being and believed that a person was a true human being only after death, after laying aside the physical body and becoming a pneumatic being.

That is why initiation into the Mysteries in ancient times was closely connected with the development of humility regarding human consciousness on earth. Initiation did not make people arrogant and proud because it did not give them the feeling that they were fully human in the true sense of the word. Instead, pupils were made to feel that they were merely candidates for true humanity, and that they had to use their earthly life wisely in order to become fully human after death.

According to this Mystery wisdom, then, people living on earth were not considered a true expression of full humanity. Thanks to their intellectuality and freedom, the ancient Greeks and the civilizations under their influence eventually sensed that the true human essence was streaming from the life after death into human beings on earth. According to the point of view prevailing in ancient Greece, individual persons did not represent the full unfolding of the human essence, but they made visible, so to speak, the work of the stream from the supersensible. People then saw the streaming in of the supra-earthly into the earthly realm in a person's whole physiognomy, way of acting, and overall figure, and they revered it.

All this changed in the more recent phase of human evolution; now we have the noble task of becoming aware of our humanity. Our task on earth is to represent the true human essence as fully as possible. We, too, are faced with the challenge to know ourselves. Because of our intellectual consciousness, we can take hold of the inner force of pure thinking and the inner soul condition of freedom in the process of self-knowledge. We can behold the human being with our soul's eye, so to speak. However, being able to know ourselves to a certain extent should not make us arrogant. We have to be aware at every moment that we have to struggle for our true freedom. We have to be aware that in our passions and emotions, in our feelings and sentiments, we are dependent on the subhuman.

People in ancient times could perceive this subhuman realm vividly in their picture consciousness. In fact, in those times people greatly appreciated the significance of the subhuman for their knowledge. They believed that the true human being was not to be found on earth because, as an intellectual being, this true human being would have had to be understood with intellectual cognition. Only the subhuman realm can be perceived with the nonintellectual, pictorial consciousness. Only when intellectual capacities—which live in a free inner soul condition as I described in *The Philosophy of Freedom*—are developed into conscious and exact clairvoyance will self-knowledge be possible also in regard to the other parts of our being, apart from pure intellectual thinking and the free impulses of willing.[2]

Through such a higher consciousness—an imaginative, inspired, and intuitive consciousness—we can see ourselves apart from the intellect as members of the supersensible world. Then we realize that although we are fully human— as our self-knowledge shows us—our full humanity demands that we continuously perfect our humanity. That is why we cannot develop the kind of humility people had to have in ancient civilizations. Their humility grew out of the realization that during life in the physical body people were not fully human, were not fully unfolding their human dignity and value, but were only on the way to becoming true human beings. During life on earth, they could only prepare themselves for the consciousness and freedom they were to have immediately after death.

Having gone through the intermediary stage of Greek civilization in earlier incarnations, we modern people must take care not to forget to be fully human in our physical body between birth and death. For it is granted to us to work out inwardly what has entered our earthly life from our pre-earthly existence. We *can* become fully human on earth, and therefore we must take on that difficult task.

This change is expressed in the development of our religious consciousness. In our last talk, we heard that in ancient times people mostly worshiped God the Father and saw Christ as the Son of God. They perceived God the Father in the substance-creating and guiding forces of the supersensible world, of which the sensory world on earth is only a pale reflection. They looked up to the cosmos and worshiped God the Father.

The candidates for initiation into the Mysteries were always aware that the greatest knowledge about the human being they could acquire was a preparation for life after death. Then, through the Mystery of Golgotha, the Son of God united Himself with earthly life, and since then human beings can develop the consciousness of St. Paul: "I have been crucified with Christ; it is no longer I who live, but Christ who lives in me." (Gal. 2:20) When we allow Christ to come alive in us, and orient our inner activity so that the purpose and life of Christ flows and breathes through us, then we can begin to sense the stream that has come to us from our pre-earthly life and take it into ourselves during this life on earth. The first, elementary sign of taking this stream into ourselves is to say to ourselves: At a certain point in life, we begin to feel something livening up and bursting forth within us, something that until then existed beneath the threshold of our consciousness. It is only now that we notice its existence. Now it rises up! It fills us with inner light that is also inner warmth. And because this inner life, this inner warmth, this inner light, has arisen within us only in the course of our life after birth, we now know more about earthly life than we did by nature. We come to know something during our earthly life that arises from our humanness.

When we feel this rising light and life and the love rising up within us, and identify them as Christ living and working in us, then we become inwardly strengthened to understand in our free soul the life after death as the fully human one. Thus, the Mystery of Golgotha and the Christ-Impulse are intimately connected with our attainment of a consciousness of freedom, a consciousness that can also fill our thinking with inner life and inner warmth, thus keeping it from becoming abstract and dead. This shows clearly the full significance and importance of Christ within us. We need to see this in connection with the demand made on all people at all times, even today: "Know yourself. Fructify your inner being to become fully human."

Here you can see the difference between what has to live in our soul and what was needed in former times. In fact, we can look at human beings over a large span of time in the same way we do at insects. As animals live integrated into the course of the year, so we should live within the history of our planet earth. We have to realize that, just as there is a springtime for the insects, so there once was a time when we had an ancient, instinctive clairvoyance accompanied by unfreedom and an imaginative consciousness. We were then unable to know ourselves. Instead, there was the awareness that we would not be fully human until after we had passed through the portal of death. And then, just as there are summer and fall for the insects, so for us there was the epoch of Greek antiquity. That was the transition to our period, where the task for our soul is to fulfill, in a certain sense, the command "Know yourself" here on earth. As a result, our soul will achieve a higher stage of development after death than people were able to reach in ancient times when they became fully human only after death.

In those ancient times, human beings had the task of being candidates for becoming fully human while here on earth. We now have the task of becoming fully human already here on earth so that we can reach higher stages of development after death. If people in ancient times did not live their lives on earth properly, they were in danger of not attaining full humanity. We modern people face a different problem. If we do not achieve full humanity here on earth, we, in fact, repudiate it and condemn ourselves to descending further into the subhuman realm after death. If people in ancient times did not become candidates for full humanity, they simply had left something undone. However, if we do not strive to become fully human on earth, we destroy something for all of humanity, because we then repudiate humanness; people in ancient times merely missed it.

This is how we have to think at our higher stage of development if we want to live consciously in the world similarly to how animals, on a lower level, live in their world—instinctively. Otherwise we fall prey to chaos, something that cannot happen to animals because of their instincts.

We have to learn from anthroposophy to be really human so that we do not experience the disgrace of being less than the animals although the gods have destined us for something higher. After all, animals cannot fail to participate in the harmony of the universe; however, if we do not want to think as I have indicated and to bring the right consciousness to bear at the right times, then we turn the cosmic harmony into something dissonant and, so to speak, fall into cosmic disgrace.

We must learn to unite our feeling life with our intellectual life. We must become aware that it can be a disgrace not to strive for the kind of insight that makes us fully human—a disgrace in the eyes of the gods.

February 3, 1923

THE HUMAN BEING IN WAKING AND IN SLEEPING

PART I

TODAY I would like to begin by telling you about an episode in nineteenth century philosophy to give you an idea of the great changes that have taken place in the soul life of Western humanity. As I have often emphasized, people nowadays are convinced that human beings have always thought, felt, and perceived the same way we do now. Any differences corresponded to the childlike level of development in earlier times; of course, our thinking has now reached the level of maturity. To arrive at real insight into the human being we must be able to understand how people thought in former times. Then we will not feel so proud of what fills our souls. When we realize how completely the ideas and thoughts of educated people have changed in the course of just a few decades, we will get an idea of the radical change that has taken place in human soul life over long periods of time. We spoke about this change yesterday.

One of the best known Hegelian scholars of the nineteenth century was Karl Rosenkranz.[1] After stints in several other places, he was professor of philosophy at the Königs-

berg University for many years. Although he was a Hegelian, Rosenkranz's understanding of Hegel was colored,
first, by his thorough study of Kant—he looked at Hegel
through Kantian glasses, so to speak—and, second, by his
study of Protestant theology.[2] Thus, in this man of the mid-
nineteenth century, Protestant theology, Kantianism, and
Hegelianism merged.

Hegelianism pretty much disappeared from the world
view of educated circles in the last third of the nineteenth
century in Central Europe; therefore we can hardly imagine
how deeply rooted in Hegelianism educated people still
were in the 1840s. That is why it will be difficult for us to
imagine what a soul such as that of Karl Rosenkranz was
like. In the 1840s, Rosenkranz was a person whose thinking
conformed to what was then expected of a man who had left
behind the old, useless way of thinking, and had fallen in
with modern enlightenment—in short, a man who was not
superstitious according to the definition of that word in the
1840s. We can think of Rosenkranz, then, as having reached
the highest level of education of his time.

One day in 1843, Rosenkranz was going for a walk and
met a man named Bon with whom he had such an interesting conversation that he later wrote it down.[3] Bon was a
native of Thuringia, and he was by no means as much a
product of his time as Rosenkranz was. For his part, Bon
probably thought that Rosenkranz had been taken in by the
latest ideas. He probably took Rosenkranz for a man who
was in a way unprejudiced yet could no longer understand
the good old wisdom that Bon himself still had.

In 1843, as I said, these two men had a conversation. Bon
had been educated at the University of Erlangen where he
had studied mainly with the philosopher Schubert.[4] Now
Schubert had a touch of pietism, but he was still full of the

17

older wisdom that placed great emphasis on being able to penetrate the essence of the human being by means of special, dreamlike states of consciousness. Schubert had great respect for this traditional wisdom. He believed that if one could not bring to life something of the good old wisdom in one's own inner life, then even the modern wisdom would not really teach one anything about the human being. The works of Schubert are very interesting in this regard. Schubert liked to immerse himself in the many revelations of dream life as well as in abnormal soul conditions, or, as we would say today, in the soul conditions of a genuine medium—one who is not a fraud—and in the kind of clairvoyance that has been preserved from ancient times as an atavism. In short, Schubert liked to study the abnormal and not-fully-awake states of soul. That is how he tried to gain insight into the human being.

Well, Bon was one of Schubert's students. After his studies, Bon came here to Switzerland and took up a spiritual stream of which most present-day Swiss probably know nothing at all. I am referring to the philosophy of Gichtel, which Bon then adopted.[5] I do not know whether many Swiss people of our time realize that Gichtelianism was fairly widespread not only in the rest of Europe—for instance, in the mid-nineteenth century it had become established in Holland—but was also quite well known here in Switzerland. Gichtelianism was what had remained of the teaching of Jakob Böhme throughout the eighteenth century and even in the nineteenth century.[6] Jakob Böhme's teaching spread throughout many countries, including Switzerland, in the form in which Gichtel presented it, and this was how Bon met it.

Well, Rosenkranz had read a great deal, and even though his Kantianism, Hegelianism, and Protestant theology did not allow him to find his way in inward activity into something like Jakob Böhme's teaching or even into Gichtel's watered-down version of it, he did at least understand its terminology. He was interested to hear such a strange person as the Gichtelian Bon speak.

As I said, Rosenkranz wrote down the conversation that took place in 1843. At first, they spoke about a subject that did not have any unduly incomprehensible aspects for Kantians or for nineteenth-century Hegelians. In the course of their talk, Rosenkranz said it was really unfortunate that all sorts of outer disturbances could keep one from really thinking deeply about a problem. In Rosenkranz's words we can already feel what appeared later to a far greater degree, namely, the nervousness that is so common in our age. We only need to remember that among the many clubs and associations that were formed before the war in Central Europe there was one that originated in Hanover dedicated to the prevention of noise. Its members wanted to lobby for laws against noise so that they could sit quietly and think in the evenings without being disturbed, for example, by a neighboring inn. There were newspaper articles propagating this association for the prevention of noise. The idea of founding such a club is, of course, a typical expression of our nervous age.

We can feel from Karl Rosenkranz's comment that all kinds of things going on around them could disturb people when they wanted to think or write a book. You can practically feel the nervousness. It seems Bon had real understanding for the complaint of a man who wants to think without being disturbed. He told Rosenkranz that he could give him some good advice in this matter. And then Bon suggested that Rosenkranz practice unreceptiveness.

Rosenkranz was thunderstruck and could not believe his

ears: he was supposed to practice unreceptiveness! He did not really understand this. So Bon explained to Rosenkranz what he meant by unreceptiveness. He said that Rosenkranz should strive to become firm in himself so that the "turba" of the other processes around him did not disturb his own constellation, so that he could maintain the "pure tincture" of his own "astrum."

Well, Bon had learned from the Swiss Gichtelians to say that one should strive not to be disturbed in one's own constellation by the turba of the processes in one's surroundings so that the pure tincture of one's own astrum could remain intact. As I said, Rosenkranz understood these terms. I think nowadays not everyone understands them, not even all the people who think themselves very learned.

What did the Gichtelian Bon actually mean? Well, you have to keep in mind that Bon was rooted in ideas that came down from Jakob Böhme. I told you a bit about Böhme recently; I said that he collected traditional folk wisdom, from which he learned much that people nowadays would refuse to accept. This folk wisdom has been preserved in some contemplative people in expressions such as the one I quoted from Bon. Back then, people still connected something that was in a certain sense inwardly alive with such expressions, because they still had traditions going back to what their ancestors had taken in through ancient clairvoyance.

That kind of clairvoyance was based on forces coming from the person's bodily nature. Yet, this should not lead us to say that this ancient clairvoyance lived in the physical body, for then we would fail to realize that everything corporeal is permeated by spirit. Actually, the ancient clairvoyants drew the dreamlike images they saw before their soul out of the forces of their corporeality. The forces pulsating in the blood and the breath and even those living in the changing substances of their body rose up like spiritual steam, so to speak, and gave the ancient clairvoyants the grandiose world pictures I have often described to you. Ancient clairvoyance was actually drawn up out of the body.

The ancients gave the name "tincture" to what was revealed when the clairvoyant felt the whole world bathed in a violet light and himself living in a violet cloud in this light, and felt at one with himself. Clairvoyants felt this tincture as their own, as connected to their organism. They felt it as their very own astrum. The Gichtelian Bon called this inwardness, which was drawn up out of the body, the pure tincture of one's own astrum.

But the time had already come—actually it had already begun much earlier—when human beings could no longer draw up such things out of their corporeality. The ancient clairvoyance had long since ceased to be suited to people. That is why people like Jakob Böhme or Gichtel felt that it was difficult to bring such old ideas and images to life for oneself. People had lost the ability to live in these old images, since they practically vanished as soon as they appeared. People felt uncertain about them and tried as hard as they could to hold on to these fleeting inner images, which in those days could still be evoked by the inner sound of the old words. Once people experienced this pure tincture of their astrum in themselves, they felt that anything coming from the outside would immediately push away their inner images. The disturbing influence that lived spiritually in things and events around them was called turba.

The state of soul people achieved by immersing themselves deeply into the inner sound of the old words was not to be disturbed by this turba—after all, people wanted to hold fast to their human essence by preserving this traditional inner life. This is why they strove not to take in anything from the outside and to live only in themselves. They became unreceptive in order not to have to let in anything from the outside.

This unreceptiveness, this living in oneself as I have just explained it, is what Bon recommended to Rosenkranz. You see, here we can get a glimpse of the soul life of a very ancient time, a soul life that existed still in the Gichtelian circles in the middle of the nineteenth century though it was already in decline and fading away. But this soul life had once been an inner participation in the divine-spiritual world through dreamlike, clairvoyant pictures that made people feel more as heavenly beings than earthly ones.

This ancient state of soul was possible only because people had not yet developed the clear thinking we now have. Actually, people do not yet have much of a sense for this pure thinking of modern times, which was first developed in the natural sciences and discussed for the first time in *The Philosophy of Freedom*.[7]

Let us look at an area of the natural sciences where we can see particularly clearly what I will be talking about, namely, astronomy. Under the influence of Copernicus, astronomy has simply become cosmic mechanics, a kind of description of the world machinery.[8] Prior to this, people still believed that spiritual beings were embodied in the stars. Medieval scholasticism spoke of the spiritual being of the stars, of the intelligences inhabiting the stars and being embodied in them, and so on. The idea that everything out there is merely matter, empty of thought, and that human beings alone have thoughts about it all has come only rather recently. In earlier times, people used to form pictures that were connected with what they believed about stars and constellations. They saw them as imbued with inner life. Back then, people related to the world not through pure thinking; they were connected with it through something of a living soul nature. People then gradually developed pure thinking.

Of course, in ancient times people also had thoughts, but they received them together with their clairvoyance. They received their clairvoyant pictures from the world around them, and then they derived their thoughts from their clairvoyance. They did not yet derive pure thoughts directly from external objects. The characteristic feature of modern times is that human beings are learning to comprehend the world through their pure thinking, which is developed further in the process.

Bon's suggestion can be traced back to people who did not experience sleep as we do. We merely think, and we experience sleep as a state of unconsciousness interrupted by dreams, of which we do not think very highly—and rightly so, for due to the modern constitution of our soul, dreams do not mean much. As a rule, they are only reminiscences of our inner or outer life, and their content is of little value and use. Thus, the main characteristic of sleep is unconsciousness. This was not always the case. Jakob Böhme himself certainly experienced a kind of sleep during which his consciousness was filled with real insights into world mysteries.

People like Jakob Böhme and Gichtel were still able to enter into that state of soul through working at it diligently. They realized that when we look at sensory objects with our eyes, then use other senses to perceive the world, and then use our thoughts to further understand what our senses perceive, we can come to many interesting insights into the world. Yet, the true mysteries of the world will not be revealed to us in this way. All we will get is just an outer picture of the world.

Both Jakob Böhme and Gichtel knew states of consciousness in which they were neither sleeping nor merely dreaming; rather, their consciousness was filled with insights into the true mysteries of the world that are hidden behind the sense world. In fact, they valued these insights more than what their senses and intellect disclosed to them. Mere thinking was not yet of great significance for these people.

They also knew the counterpart to this, namely, that human beings can perceive without using their bodies. For in those states of consciousness that were neither sleeping nor dreaming, they also knew that their essential being had, for the most part, torn itself free of their body but had taken the force of the blood and the breathing with it. Thus, they knew that human beings are inwardly connected with the world, but while they are awake, their body obscures this connection.

However, when people become to a certain extent independent of their bodies in the waking state, they can gain insights into the mysteries of the world through the subtler forces of their bodies. These forces were drawn up out of the body by clairvoyance, as I have explained. From such special conditions of sleep, people learned what sleep actually is. Jakob Böhme and Gichtel realized that when they were asleep, the finer members of their being were outside in the subtler elements of nature. They felt themselves immersed in these subtler elements of nature. When they woke up, they realized that their subtler being, which had been in the finer elements of nature during sleep—even during sleep without consciousness—was living in them also when they were awake. They understood that they were filling their body with their subtler being when they were feeling and thinking—of course, back then thinking was not yet pure thinking. They knew that this subtler humanness lived in the pictures they were forming while they were thinking.

In brief, in those days people saw real meaning in the statement that what we are in sleep continues to live in us when we are awake. In fact, they felt this state of sleep continue to pulsate in them as a kind of soul blood when they were fully awake and conscious. People like Jakob Böhme and Gichtel realized that even when they were awake they were still continuing to sleep because what happened in them during sleep continued in the waking state.

This is a very different feeling from the one we have—we who have moved on to pure thinking, to pure intellectual thinking. When we wake up in the morning, we usually draw a clear line between what we were in sleep and what we are in the waking state. In a sense, we take nothing from sleep into our waking life. What we were in sleep ceases to exist the moment we begin to wake up. Indeed, modern humanity has outgrown the states of consciousness that were still alive for people like Bon. In the process, modern humanity has brought to full realization something that has been present in rudimentary form since the first third of the fifteenth century. This full realization was achieved through the transition to purely intellectual thinking in waking life. That is what dominates all people nowadays. We do not think in pictures anymore. Instead, pictures are generally thought to be mythology, as I explained yesterday. People nowadays think only in thoughts and they sleep in nothingness.

In fact, that we nowadays sleep in nothingness has a profound significance. The statement, "I sleep in nothingness," would not have made sense to Jakob Böhme, but it has meaning for us. We are not nothing when we are asleep; we keep our I and our astral body during sleep. So we are not nothing, but we tear ourselves away from the sense-perceptible world, which we comprehend with our intellect when we are awake. At the same time, when we are asleep, we also tear ourselves away from the world Jakob Böhme and others perceived in abnormal states of consciousness with the subtler forces of their physical and etheric bodies, and which they took with them into sleep.

In other words, when we are asleep, we tear ourselves away not only from the world of the senses but also from the world of ancient clairvoyance. And the world we then enter between falling asleep and waking up is a world of the future; therefore, we cannot perceive it. It is the world into which our earth will be transformed in those stages of development I have called Jupiter, Venus, and Vulcan in my book, *An Outline of Occult Science*.[9] Thus, we modern people who are drilled to think intellectually live in nothingness when we are sleeping. We *are* not nothing, as I have to stress again and again, but we *live in nothingness* because we cannot yet experience the world we live in, which is the world of the future; it is as yet a nothing to us.

However, it is precisely through our ability to sleep in nothingness that our freedom is guaranteed. For from the moment of falling asleep until we wake up, we are becoming accustomed to being free of the world and living in nothingness. Thus, it is when we are asleep that we become independent. It is very important to realize that the way we sleep guarantees us our freedom. The ancient clairvoyants, who still perceived the old world but not the future one, could not become completely free human beings because the process of perception made them dependent.

However, resting in nothingness while being asleep makes people of our times really free.

Thus, we have seen two contrasting, complementary pictures of modern humanity. First, when we are awake, we live in thoughts that are purely thoughts and nothing else. These thoughts no longer contain pictures in the old sense (which, in any case, people now regard as myths). Second, when we are asleep, we live in nothingness, and in that way we free ourselves from the world and become conscious of our freedom. The images in our thoughts can no longer compel us because they are mere pictures. Just as mirror images cannot compel us to do anything and cannot cause any events, so the pictures of things we have in our thoughts cannot force us to act.

Therefore, when we take hold of moral impulses with our pure thinking, we act upon them as free beings. No emotion, passion, or inner bodily process can compel us to act upon the moral impulses we can understand with our pure thoughts. At the same time, we are able to act on these mental images, these pure thoughts because during sleep we are free from all natural laws in our body. During sleep we become truly free souls that can act on the "unreality" of our thoughts. In contrast, people in ancient times remained dependent on the world even in sleep, and therefore they were not able to act on "unreal" impulses.

Let us look more closely at these two aspects of modern humanity. We can have pure thoughts that are purely intellectual, and we live in our sleep in nothingness; there we are real, but the world around us reveals nothing to us. Now comes the crux of the matter: You see, it is inherent in our nature that, as a result of everything we have gone through, we have become inwardly weak-willed. Of course, people nowadays do not want to admit this, but it is nevertheless true that we have become inwardly weak in our willpower.

This can be understood from a historical perspective. We need only look at the great spiritual movements that spread in earlier times to see the kind of will impulses the founders of religions, for example, worked with. This kind of inner will impulse has been lost to modern humanity. That is why people nowadays allow the outer world to teach them what to think. They study nature and develop their purely intellectual thoughts based on the natural processes and beings they perceive, as though their inner being were really only a mirror reflecting the world. Indeed, people have become so weak that they are terribly afraid when someone produces thoughts out of himself rather than merely "reading" them in nature. Thus, pure thinking initially developed in modern humanity in a completely passive way.

This is not meant as criticism, for if humanity had right away made the transition to actively producing pure thinking, all kinds of impure fantasies from the past would have entered into pure thinking. Humanity has certainly learned a valuable lesson by allowing itself to be seduced by grandiose philistines, such as Bacon of Verulam, into developing concepts and ideas based on the outer world, into letting the outer world dictate everything to them. Gradually, people have become accustomed to not living in concepts, ideas, and thinking, and to letting the outer world hand them their thinking, so to speak. For some people, this process is direct; they study nature or historical documents, for example, and that is where they get their thoughts about nature or history. These thoughts then live in them. But most people get their concepts in school; their concepts are drilled into them.

Nowadays, people are flooded from earliest childhood

with concepts that have been developed passively on the basis of the outer world. In this respect, modern people are actually like a sack that is open on the side. They take things in from nature and mirror them inside. These mirror images, then, are their ideas. Actually, their soul is merely filled up with concepts of nature. If people nowadays were to trace their concepts to their source, they would soon find that what I told you is true.

Ever since the fifteenth century, people have been taught this passivity of thinking, and now they consider it almost a sin to be inwardly active and create one's own thoughts. Of course, we cannot create thoughts about nature by ourselves; we would only pollute nature with all sorts of fantastic ideas if we tried to do that. Yet, we have the source of thinking within us. We can think thoughts of our own; in fact, we can imbue the thoughts we already have with inner reality. This can happen when we have enough will to push our night being into our waking life, to think not merely passively but rather to insert our being, which has become independent during sleep, into our thoughts. This is possible only with pure thoughts.

My main reason for writing *The Philosophy of Freedom* was to explain that we can insert our I-being into our modern thinking. At the time, I could not express it in the same words as I do now, but it really is true that when we are asleep, we free our I-being, and then we can insert it into our pure thinking. We become aware of our I-being in pure thinking when we live actively in our thoughts.

Now, let us assume anthroposophy were presented in the same way as the modern sciences. People then would take in anthroposophy in their usual manner, namely, through passive thinking. Of course, all that is needed to understand anthroposophy is sound common sense; one does not have to accept it on faith. Anybody with sound common sense can understand it. Nevertheless, if we presented anthroposophy just like the natural sciences, people would understand it only passively, just as they do in their thoughts about outer nature.

Of course, there are people who claim to have derived their thoughts from anthroposophical research. But they say they themselves cannot stand up for these thoughts because they have merely taken them in. Similarly, many people often say they have assimilated some ideas of spiritual science. We often hear people stress that the natural sciences say such and such, while spiritual science says this or that. What does it mean when people claim to have heard something from spiritual science? It means that the persons in question reveal that they are stuck in passive thinking and want to take in spiritual science only with this passive thinking. However, as soon as people decide to create in themselves the thoughts anthroposophical research gives to them, they will become able to defend the truth of these thoughts with their whole personality for, in the process, they will have experienced the first stage of truth.

In other words, people nowadays generally are not yet able to use the strength of their will to pour the independent reality they experience during sleep into the thoughts of their waking life. People who want to be anthroposophists— and not simply accept anthroposophical thoughts passively but really assimilate them—must pour what they have been during their dreamless sleep into the pure thoughts of anthroposophy with the help of their strong will. Those people will then have reached the first stage of what we can legitimately call clairvoyance. Then they live clairvoyantly in the thoughts of anthroposophy.

Anthroposophical books must be read with a strong will,

and we must bring more than just our waking life to them. We must not read anthroposophical books in the way we usually read: intermittently, every day only a little bit. Generally, people read only with their waking life. Of course, that is good enough for reading Gustav Freytag or Dickens or Emerson, but not for reading anthroposophical books.[10]

To read anthroposophical books, we really must enter into them with our whole being. Since we are unconscious during sleep and have no thoughts then—though our will is, of course, still there—we must put our whole will into the reading of anthroposophical books. If you make the contents of an anthroposophical book the object of your will, then you will become immediately clairvoyant, at least in your thoughts, through this exercise of your will. You see, this will still has to enter those who represent our anthroposophy. If this will completely permeates and electrifies those who represent anthroposophy, then anthroposophy will be presented to the world in the right way. This does not require any magic but only a forceful will that brings more than one's waking life to bear on anthroposophical books. These days people do not even use all of their waking consciousness to read. Of course, it is enough to activate a few small bits and pieces, a few minutes, so to speak, of waking life to comprehend what is contained in newspapers; it does not take a whole day of our waking life. However, anthroposophical books come alive for us only if we immerse ourselves in them with our complete being.

This must be kept in mind, especially by those who want to be leading figures in the Anthroposophical Society. For it is extremely detrimental to this society when anthroposophy is proclaimed by people who cannot stand up for it. We need to find the way from a merely passive, intellectual experiencing of anthroposophical truths to an immersion in them with our whole being. Then anthroposophical teaching will no longer be presented in a deadbeat and feeble way with phrases like, "Anthroposophical sources have assured us that . . . ." Instead, people will be able to proclaim anthroposophical truths out of their own experience, at least in the most accessible areas, such as medicine, physiology, biology, and the social sphere.

While we cannot yet reach the sphere of the higher hierarchies on that first level of clairvoyance, nevertheless we can make the spirit in our immediate surroundings the subject of our state of soul. It is a matter of will in the most comprehensive sense whether or not there will be people in our Anthroposophical Society who can give testimony—and we need a valid, living testimony based on their own direct experience of a living source of truth—of the inner truth of anthroposophy.

In addition, there must be personalities in the Anthroposophical Society who, if I may use the paradoxical expression, have a certain amount of goodwill for the will. These days, people talk about any arbitrary wish as "will," but a wish is not the same as will. Some people wish for a particular matter to turn out in such and such a way. That is not will. Will is an active force, and that is largely lacking nowadays. People of our time generally do not have it. However, it must not be lacking in the Anthroposophical Society. There, a strong will must be anchored in calm enthusiasm. That is one of the necessary conditions for the life of the Anthroposophical Society.

February 4, 1923

THE HUMAN BEING IN WAKING AND IN SLEEPING PART II

AS WE have discussed before, we must understand the evolution of humanity in order to be imbued with the consciousness we need to be human beings in the true sense of the word.

In the first lecture of this series, I used an analogy to show the importance of a consciousness of time. I explained that insects go through certain metamorphoses in harmony with the course of the year. They follow this course even in their physical form, and undergo in each season the bodily processes specific to it. Their whole life cycle is closely connected with the cycle of the year. We must find a way to enter similarly but consciously into the whole evolution of the earth, the whole history of the earth. We must know how our soul experiences had to be constituted in ancient times, how they had to be in the times since then, and how they need to be today.

In ancient epochs of human evolution, humanity received strength for knowledge and for life from the Mysteries. Those who were to be initiated into the Mysteries had to realize that the exercises they were about to undergo would finally lead them to an experience of death. They knew that they had to pass consciously through death during their earthly life in order to understand their immortal, eternal being. This was the secret at the core of the ancient Mysteries: to arrive at a vital conviction of one's immortal being through a conscious experience of death.

In our recent talks we have seen the reason for this. In those ancient times, human beings had no other way to gain self-knowledge than to think of what would happen to them immediately after death. Back then, people were free thinking beings like us only after death. Only after death did people in ancient times consider themselves independent beings, autonomous individualities. The ancient sages told their students to look beyond death if they wanted to know what a true human being is. They had to experience a reflection of death in the Mysteries to become convinced of their eternal life and immortal being. Essentially, then, to seek the Mysteries was to seek death in order to find life.

Things have changed; people are different nowadays. What people in ancient times experienced after death, namely, becoming thinking and free beings in their own right, we now have to achieve in the time between birth and death. But how can we do this? As we gain more and more self-knowledge, we first of all must get to know our thoughts. However, our thoughts, particularly those developed since the first third of the fifteenth century, since the time of Nicholas of Cusa, are actually dead thoughts; they are corpses.[1] What lived in them was alive in our pre-earthly existence. Before we descended to earth as soul-spiritual beings, we lived a spiritual life. With the beginning of our earthly life, this spiritual life died, and we now experience this dead spiritual life in us as our thinking.

The first thing we must realize is that while we can arrive at true self-knowledge in our age—that is, we can know ourselves as soul-spiritual beings—the object of our self-knowledge is dead; it is a spiritual corpse. Something coming from the will, which is actually in nothingness during our sleep and yet anchored in the astral body and the I, must flow into this dead element. The I must stream into the dead thoughts and bring them to life.

That is why in ancient times the candidates' inner life was carefully calmed down during initiation. In a sense, the ancient initiation was actually a kind of soothing of the candidates' inner forces and capacities. Basically, the candidates underwent a training that led to a soothing of their inner excitement, as it were, to an appeasing of the inner emotionalism of everyday life. As a result, what filled their whole being in their ordinary life, the divine-spiritual forces that live and weave throughout the cosmos, was subdued. The candidates could then sink into a kind of sleep. In this state of semiconsciousness dimmed almost to the level of sleep, they could then evoke what is otherwise experienced only after death: peaceful thinking and awareness of their own individuality. In a sense, the ancient initiation was a system for soothing and calming down.

The longing to be soothed and calmed down has largely persisted into our time. People feel good when they are given the ancient principles of initiation. But this is no longer appropriate for modern human beings. In our time, we can approach initiation only when we are profoundly and intensely convinced that we find our thinking when we look into ourselves, that this thinking is dead, and that therefore we do not need to look for death any longer. We bear death within us in our soul-spiritual being. While the candidates of the Mysteries in ancient times had to be brought to the stage where they experienced death, modern candidates increasingly have to realize that they have death in their soul-spiritual life, that they bear death within them and, therefore, do not need to look for it. On the contrary, they have to bring their dead thoughts to life through inner, creative will.

This bringing to life of our dead thoughts is the aim of everything I have presented in my book *Knowledge of the Higher Worlds*.[2] This book is intended to help us let our will burst forth into our soul life so that we can wake up. Ancient initiation had to be a kind of lulling to sleep, but modern initiation must be a kind of awakening. What we experience unconsciously during sleep must be carried into the innermost core of our soul life. We must inwardly wake ourselves up, as it were, through our own activity.

To be able to do this, we must understand the concept of sleep in all its ramifications. We must be aware of the current anthroposophical understanding of sleep. For example, let us compare two people, one who knows nothing about what anthroposophy teaches and one who has taken in anthroposophy not only by passively listening or reading, but with real inner interest. The one who does not know anthroposophy is like a sleeper compared to the other who has been awakened by it—similar to how we wake up in the morning when we reenter our physical body after the unconsciousness of sleep. We will have the right attitude to anthroposophy and the right orientation in the Anthroposophical Society only when we see it as giving us something that is like our waking up in the morning.

In other words, we can compare learning about anthroposophy with the transition from the unconsciousness of sleep to a new perception of the outer world. Descending into our physical body when we wake up, in a sense, gives us a world—not just knowledge, but a world. In the same way, becoming deeply absorbed with anthroposophy also gives us a world. It gives us knowledge that is at the same time also a world, and we can awaken to this world. As long as we see anthroposophy as just another world view, we do not have the right attitude to it. We develop the right attitude only when we feel ourselves awakening in the process of becoming anthroposophists. We are actually waking up when we realize that the concepts and ideas the world has given us are dead, mere corpses of thoughts and ideas, but that anthroposophy will awaken them for us.

If you understand this correctly, you will be able to rise above the things that are usually said against anthroposophy. People often say that those who are not anthroposophists can really learn something in the world these days because they obtain evidence to help them prove their conclusions about things. Anthroposophy, on the other hand, is said to make claims that remain unproved. However, most people do not know how things really stand with their so-called proofs; for if they did, they would have to realize that all the natural laws and all the thoughts we have developed based on the world are, in effect, dead. People would find this out if they experienced their thoughts properly. What is being proven to us is actually dead and therefore cannot be understood. Only when we understand this can we realize that we do not understand precisely what was being proved to us. Similarly, we do not understand a corpse because it is nothing but the remains of a living person. We can understand the corpse only when we know what it was like while still imbued with life.

Thus, we have to realize that what is considered proven truth can, in fact, not be understood at all if we consider it more deeply. Indeed, what our civilization offers will be illumined for our understanding only when it catches fire from the spark of anthroposophy. If a scientist told us that he can prove his science but that we have no proofs for our knowledge, then the right answer would be that while he certainly can prove everything in his way, we will not understand what he has proven until we bring the light of anthroposophy to bear upon it. That is what an anthroposophist would reply to a nonanthroposophist out of a heart brimming with living spiritual life. Anthroposophists would have to say that the scientist is lulling himself to sleep with his knowledge about nature. In fact, the scientist will have to admit that there are limits to his knowledge and that he cannot even approach the spiritual realm with his science. We anthroposophists can tell scientists that while they justify their sleep with a theory, we want to refute this justification of their sleep by waking them up.

I mentioned this also in the first chapter of my book *Riddles of the Soul* as well as in many lectures.[3] I explained that those people who remain stuck at the level of present-day civilization actually admit that there are many insurmountable limits to knowledge. This puts their minds at ease, but it also means that they do not want to wake up at all but want to stay asleep. To reach the spiritual world in the way appropriate for our time, we must struggle inwardly with the tasks of our soul at the very point where other people come up against the limits of knowledge. As we begin our struggle with the ideas that demarcate those limits, gradually and step-by-step a view into the spiritual world will open up. To achieve this, we must take what anthroposophy offers in the way it is intended.

When you read the first chapter of *Riddles of the Soul*, regardless of how imperfectly it may be written, you will see my intention in writing it. I wanted to help people realize that if they remain stuck at the level of our present civilization, the world will be boarded up for them, so to speak. With the natural sciences we can progress only so far, then we come to where the world is as though boarded up. That chapter was my attempt to clear away the boards. If you have the feeling that you are pulling away the boards that have enclosed the world for centuries now, when you can regard the words in my book as tools for this pulling away, then you really approach the soul-spiritual. Most people have only an unconscious feeling that chapters such as this are written with pen and ink. Indeed, they are not written with a pen, but with soul tools intended to tear away those boards, that is, to clear away the limits of natural science through inner soul work. When you read such a chapter, you must work too and be active in your soul.

Sometimes people get strange ideas from reading anthroposophical books. I can understand these ideas, and usually do not refute them because they are of a certain value for the individual having them. For example, concerning my book *An Outline of Occult Science*, some people have had the idea to illustrate it so that it could be presented in pictures, and they thought they would be doing the book a favor with this.[4] In fact, people have even shown me samples of such pictures. I have nothing against that; if the sample pictures are good, we can admire them, and it is certainly nice to paint such pictures. But what is the longing that gave rise to this idea? It is the longing to take away the most important thing that can be developed through reading *An Outline of Occult Science*, and instead to present people with pictures that once again board up the world for them.

What matters most in reading this book is not to rebel against what civilization has brought us—in spite of the decline of our language and the awful state of writing and publishing nowadays—but to accept it in such way that, in reading, we overcome all this and go beyond it to creating on our own the pictures that are presented in the awful printer's ink in the book. The more unique and individual pictures each reader is able to create in his or her mind, the better. However, if somebody else draws these pictures for the readers, he boards up the world for them, so to speak. Of course, I do not want to deliver a lecture against painting what is presented in imaginations in my *An Outline of Occult Science*, but I do want to point out that everybody needs to have the experience of taking it in actively.

These things have to be understood in the right way in our time. People must realize that anthroposophy is not something they can take up the same way as other things. Rather, anthroposophy requires a change in our way of thinking and feeling—in our being. Consequently, when you hear an anthroposophical lecture on astronomy, you cannot simply compare it with ordinary astronomy, using one to substantiate or refute the other. That would not make any sense. Instead, you have to realize that you can understand the anthroposophical view of astronomy only when your thinking and feeling have changed. For example, when we see the anthroposophical view on any issue repudiated and then use the same methods as the refutation to present our counterargument, we accomplish nothing, absolutely nothing. Both sides merely argue back and forth within the same framework. That is not what it's all about. What matters is rather that anthroposophy is carried by a new life—that is indeed absolutely necessary in our time.

February 9, 1923

EARTHLY LEARNING AND HEAVENLY WISDOM: HUMAN BEINGS AS CITIZENS OF THE UNIVERSE AND HERMITS ON THE EARTH

PART I

OUR PREVIOUS talks were primarily devoted to showing how we can become aware of our place in the evolution
of humanity. Even people who do not want anything to do
with knowledge of spiritual worlds have some awareness of
our relationship to the cosmos. Today, let us look more
closely at a popular opinion about this. Even people who
base all their views of the universe on outer, sensory phe-
nomena and their interpretation by the intellect will admit
that human consciousness has changed over the course of
the past centuries. In particular, people point to the tremendous change caused by the emergence of the Copernican
world view.[1]

The world view prevailing during the centuries preceding

the Copernican world view—for example, in the era of scholasticism, which I have talked about recently—saw spiritual forces and beings present within the world of the stars. The scholastics spoke of the inhabitants of the stars who belong to hierarchies above ours in the evolution of beings. People at that time looked out into the universe, to the planets of our planetary system and to the other stars, and were aware that more than etheric-material light was streaming down. They knew that when they looked up to the stars, the spiritual beings embodied there were looking down into their souls.

Then all this changed, and when people nowadays look up at the planets and the other stars, they see above all material bodies that are permeated by ether and are floating freely in space and sending out light. It would not occur to modern people that spiritual beings of the higher hierarchies are looking at them from the stars. For modern people, the universe is devoid of soul and spirit.

In ancient times, people believed that spiritual life on earth was closely connected with that of the whole universe. To them, the creative forces in the spiritual beings of the stars were connected with the soul-spiritual and physical development of human beings on the earth. For example, in the rays of light coming to the earth from Saturn, they saw the forces stream down that influence human beings and give them the capacity to remember. They knew Jupiter was connected with spiritual beings of higher hierarchies who worked upon human beings, enabling them to develop their power of imagination. Concerning Mars, people believed that the forces of the spiritual beings of that planet endowed them with the power of reason. This is how people in earlier epochs of our evolution looked at the starry sky; to them the starry sky was the origin of what they perceived in themselves in body, soul, and spirit. They felt connected with beings of higher hierarchies, who were outwardly visible in the stars.

This view of the world disappeared with the emergence of the Copernican world view. Understandably, people had earlier considered the earth a gift of the whole cosmos because they saw that it was under the influence of an infinite number of spiritual life forces from the cosmos. For them, the earth was the focal point of the workings of countless beings. People in those times felt themselves to be citizens of the earth and at the same time citizens of the universe.

They looked up to their gods and worshipped them, and they believed that it had been the gods' intention to determine the course of human evolution on earth. They could understand the earth in its history and as the dwelling place of human beings on the basis of what they knew about the cosmos, the universe. In other words, their explanation of the earth was based on the heavens, and they believed that the gods had intended and planned the processes around them with which they knew themselves to be closely connected.

As a result of the Copernican world view, people in modern times have a very different picture of the world. They feel that the earth is an insignificant celestial body orbiting the sun. Consequently, they cannot help calling the earth a speck of dust in the universe. Based on physical size, their only criterion, people now consider all the other heavenly bodies more important than the earth. In physical size, our earth is no match for most other heavenly bodies. Thus, people see the earth only as a speck of dust in the universe, and they feel themselves to be insignificant in the cosmos, too. After all, spiritual forces no longer connect them to the universe. They find it impossible to believe that what happens on this unimportant speck of dust could in any way be connected with plans of divine beings in the cosmos. In fact, we could say that everything people used to see on earth by virtue of knowing that the heavens were inhabited by spiritual beings and forces has been lost in modern times. The universe became devoid of soul and spirit. The earth shriveled up into an insignificant bit of dust in a world without soul and spirit.

We must look at this change in the picture of the world not only from the theoretical point of view but from that of human consciousness itself. People had a different understanding of themselves when they still saw themselves as living on an earth on which countless spiritual beings worked, manifesting and realizing their plans in human beings. Obviously, believing the universe devoid of spirit, filled only with globe-shaped, moving celestial bodies, and studying their movement and emission of light will have a different effect. Imagine what it must feel like to live on one of the smallest of the heavenly bodies in a universe devoid of soul and spirit!

Yet, this view of the world was necessary in the course of evolution. What people in ancient times knew about the heavens and their inhabitants, the divine-spiritual beings, was inspiration—it was the imagination of an ancient, dreamlike clairvoyance. This clairvoyance had descended into human beings out of the universe. We have to get a clear picture of these things. In ancient times, people saw divine-spiritual forces at work in Saturn, Jupiter, and Mars because revelations from these heavenly bodies entered into human beings and were reflected within them. Based on the cosmic influences within themselves, people knew what

streams down upon the earth from the cosmos. They understood the earth on the basis of what the heavens had given
them. People in those days looked up to their gods, and that
is how they knew who they were on the earth.

The modern picture of the world tells us none of this.
According to the modern world view, the earth has shriveled up into a speck of dust in the universe, and human
beings are small, insignificant creatures upon it. The gods
of the stars no longer tell us anything about plants, animals,
and the other kingdoms of the earth. Now we have to focus
our senses on all that exists in the mineral, plant, animal,
and human kingdoms, on what lives in winds and waves,
clouds, lightning, and thunder. We can no longer receive any
revelations about things on earth except those our senses
give us. And we can arrive at conclusions about what exists
in the universe only on the basis of what the sensory phe-
nomena on earth have revealed to us in a sensory, intellectual revelation.

This is the profound change human beings have undergone in the fifth post-Atlantean epoch, the age of the development of the consciousness soul. The forces people at one
time received from the universe that lit up again in their
souls had to be squeezed out of them. Only then could they
come to the realization that they live on a speck of dust in
the universe, and that this universe does not give them any
indications of a soul-spiritual element living within them.
They had to understand that if they wanted to experience
spirit and soul in themselves, they had to squeeze it out of
their own being. In other words, they had to renounce the
revealing forces coming to them out of the universe. Instead, they had to fill their souls out of their own efforts and
activity. They could only hope that there was something
living in what poured out of their souls, something that

would throw light on the universe from the other direction, so to speak, namely, based on the human being.

In former times, it was possible for people to learn about themselves through the revelations the universe gave them. They could see themselves as children of the heavens because the heavens were telling them that this is what they were. In modern times, people have become more or less earth hermits—they live a lonely life on a speck of dust in the universe. They have to muster all their strength to develop in their solitude within themselves what can unfold in them; they have to wait and see whether what is revealed within them will indeed give them knowledge about the universe.

For centuries, these inner revelations told people nothing about the universe. They described the mineral kingdom according to its dimensions in space and time. Then they analyzed the way it functions in geology. They described the outer sense-perceptible processes and how they take place; for example, how the plants spring up from the mineral soil of the earth. They also studied the sense-perceptible processes that take place inside animals and the human physical body. People investigated everything on earth to see what their senses could tell them about life on earth. But, above all, their senses told them nothing about their own soul and their own spirit. Out of the frame of mind accompanying the realization that human beings are hermits on the earth, living on a speck of dust in the universe, had to come the impulse to develop true humanness in free inner development. In fact, human beings had to confront the big question: "Is there really nothing in the environment our senses can see, hear, and feel and our intellect can understand that goes beyond what our senses tell us?"

Human beings have developed science. Yet, no matter

how interesting this science may be, it does not say anything about human beings; it aims rather at abstract, dead
concepts that lead to natural laws. All this does not take
human beings into account. After all, human beings are not
merely the point where all these abstract ideas meet, in
other words, a container for all the laws of nature! For these
natural laws have nothing of a soul or spirit nature about
them although they were formulated by the human spirit.

The young Goethe especially felt the mood that accompanies this outlook at a significant time in the development
of our world view.[2] He expressed his feelings in the first
version of his drama *Faust*.[3] Goethe presents Faust there as
a man who is aware of the purpose of human beings in the
cosmos and who wants to feel himself a spirit and soul
among other spirits and souls. Yet, Faust feels thrown back
by the world without spirit and soul. So he turns to ancient
revelations of mysticism and magic, opening an old book
where he finds descriptions of the beings of the higher hierarchies living in the stars and their movements—a book
that talks about heavenly forces rising and descending,
handing each other their golden urns.[4]

Such views existed at one time, but in the period in which
Goethe places Faust they no longer spoke to people. So Faust
turns from them just as Goethe turned from the ancient
explanation of the universe, which saw soul and spirit in
everything. Instead, Faust turns to the sign of the Earth
Spirit. We then read the strange words spoken by the Earth
Spirit:

In the tides of life, in action's storm,
I surge and ebb,
As cradle and grave,
as unending sea,

as constant change,
as life's incandescence,
I work at the whirring loom of time
and fashion the living garment of God.[5]

However, Goethe shows clearly that there is something wrong about the Earth Spirit appearing to Faust; he has Faust collapse under its influence. As a result, Faust is then exposed to the influence of Mephistopheles. We will have to take a kind of heretical view of much that has been said and written about *Faust* when we consider the Earth Spirit's monumental and terse words from the point of view of a concrete picture of the world and are sufficiently unbiased to come to the same judgment as Goethe did in his feelings. After all, Goethe did not stop writing after the scene with the Earth Spirit, but continued with the play. In other words, much of what is said about *Faust* definitely does not represent Goethe's actual opinion. It is mind-boggling to think of all the things that have been said about *Faust*.

People keep quoting the words Faust says to the sixteen-year old Gretchen later on in the course of the play: "Encompassing all, sustaining all.... Feeling is everything, name is but sound and smoke."[6] And they feel so tremendously philosophical, quoting all those things that are supposed to express one's own soul concepts, even though these are words with which Faust charms a teenage girl. Isn't it embarrassing to hear these charming words for a teenage girl quoted as the quintessence of a world view by people who think themselves clever? That is what unbiased observation reveals—though it is heretical.

Similar things have happened with the terse yet monumental words of the Earth Spirit: "In the tides of life, in action's storm" and so on. They are beautiful words but very general; we find in them a sort of sensory-nebulous mystical pantheism. It makes us feel hazy, doesn't it, to be confronted with these lines:

In the tides of life, in action's storm,
I surge and ebb,
As cradle and grave,
as unending sea,
as constant change,
as life's incandescence,
I work at the whirring loom of time
and fashion the living garment of God.

These lines contribute nothing to give us the faculty for concrete insight into the universe. Goethe certainly felt this, especially later on, for he did not stop at this point but wrote the "Prologue in Heaven." When we read this prologue—"In ancient rivalries with fellow spheres the sun still sings its glorious song, . . ."[7]—it reminds us much more of the heavenly forces rising and descending, passing their golden urns from hand to hand, than of the rather nebulous flowing and weaving of the Earth Spirit.

Goethe turned away from focusing on the Earth Spirit—we can't say from idolizing it, but it was something like that. In his later, more mature years, Goethe no longer considered the Earth Spirit the only one he could turn to in the character of Faust. Rather, he returned to the spirit of the great world, the spirit of the universe. Even though the Earth Spirit's words in the first version of *Faust* are beautiful and monumental, they are akin—so as not to be impolite I will call it a distant kinship—to the "Encompassing all, sustaining all" of Faust's words to young Gretchen. Why should these words not be beautiful, in spite of all this? Of course, one has to try to speak as beautifully as possible particularly to advise and charm teenage girls! So, why shouldn't Faust's words here be beautiful? However, we must realize that as a mature man Goethe no longer believed nebulous pantheism could give people a true awareness of the cosmos.

Considering Goethe's concrete way of looking at the world—concrete at least to a certain extent—we know that he would not have been able to write the role of Faust as he did if he had intended him as a representative of Western civilization in the eleventh or twelfth century. He would then have had to take another figure, whom he could never have characterized the way he did Faust. In that case, Faust would not have put away the book of Nostradamus and turned from the spirit of the great world to the Earth Spirit, for in those days people were aware that understanding themselves rightly meant seeing themselves as children of the heavens who learn about their own being from what the spirits of the heavens tell them.[8]

Faust, however, represents humanity in the sixteenth century, that is, in the fifth post-Atlantean epoch when people began to think of themselves as earth hermits living on a speck of dust in the universe. Thus, the young Goethe would not have been honest if he had had Faust turn to the spirit of the great world. As a representative of humanity, Faust could not have done that, for human beings at that time were no longer conscious of any connection to the heavenly forces, which rise and descend and hand each other their golden urns—in short, to the higher hierarchies. That connection had become obscured and virtually disappeared from consciousness altogether. Faust had to go by what he as an earth hermit could be connected to, that is, the Earth Spirit.

Faust's turning to the Earth Spirit is something tremendously grandiose in Goethe's work. It represents the change in human consciousness that took place in that epoch—the change away from the darkened heavenly forces to the Earth Spirit, a change indicated by the spirit who went through the Mystery of Golgotha. For the spirit who went through the Mystery of Golgotha united himself with the earth. By connecting himself with human evolution on the earth, this spirit gave human beings the strength to look to the spirits of the earth when they could no longer look up to the heavenly spirits. And now the spirits of the earth speak within us. In ancient times, the stars in their movements revealed the heavenly words to human souls who then could interpret and understand these heavenly words. Now, however, people have to turn to their relationship to the earth, that is, they have to ask themselves whether the genius of the earth is speaking within them.

Goethe could draw nothing more than nebulous and mystically pantheistic words from the Earth Spirit. It is right and tremendously significant that Faust turns to the Earth Spirit, but it is even more impressive that Goethe does not let that spirit say anything that can fully satisfy Faust or us. That the Earth Spirit can only stammer out the world mysteries in mystical, pantheistic formulas instead of presenting them in a clear, distinct way confirms how ingeniously Goethe made Faust a part of the epoch in which he saw Faust and himself living.

Yet, we must sense in Goethe's beautiful presentation of Faust's relationship to the Earth Spirit that this spirit will gradually become ever more understandable for human beings. We will see it in ever sharper outlines when we allow the activities of our own soul, the workings of our own spirit, to reveal to us what is in the heavens. In the ancient past, the heavens revealed to human beings what they needed to know for life on the earth; now people turn to the earth because it is, after all, a creation of the heavens. And by getting to know the genius or spirits that have their dwelling on earth we can learn something about the heavens.

This is the approach I took in my book *An Outline of Occult Science*.[9] There I put down everything we can know from within ourselves. In fact, much of the contents of this book was taken from the Earth Spirit. This spirit, however, speaks about the Saturn epoch, the Sun epoch, the Moon epoch, and the Jupiter and Venus epochs of the earth.[10] The Earth Spirit tells us what it has preserved of the universe in its memory. In ancient times, people looked out to the heavens to gain insight into the earth, but now they look into their own inner being and listen to what the Earth Spirit has to say there out of its cosmic memory. Thus, through understanding the Earth Spirit, people gain insight into the macrocosm. Of course, if we properly appreciated the significance of spiritual science and spiritual insight, then we would have to present Faust's conversation with the Earth Spirit differently than Goethe did—though Goethe's way was brilliant and ingenious at his time.

Nowadays the Earth Spirit would not speak in such general, abstract terms that express something that could just as well be a flowing wave of water. It is so mystically obscure because this flowing wave of water also sits at a loom and weaves! I know, of course, that many people love to have such vague things stirring in their soul. However, these vague things do not help us achieve the inner conscious solidity we need. Lines such as "Encompassing all, sustaining all" and "in the tides of life, in action's storm" always carry an element of reverie or intoxication; here we are always a bit beside ourselves, so to speak, and not completely anchored within ourselves. Granted, it gives people a pleasurable feeling to be a bit beside themselves; some would even prefer to be completely beside themselves all the time and to learn about the world from all sorts of ghosts.

I say this to point out that we cannot help but turn to the Earth Spirit that lives within us. After all, if we accept the modern ideas of the natural sciences as they are presented to us in our civilization, then what they give us remains abstract and leaves human consciousness cold. But if we start wrestling with these concepts, even with the abstractions of Haeckel, something quite concrete will emerge that can be experienced directly.[11] Then the great realization will come to us that the indifferent ideas of natural science are only a mask. We will have to reach the point where we realize it is the genius of the earth that is telling us what we get there. We have to listen with our whole soul to what we hear at first only with our abstract intellect. And then we will understand in a concrete way what the Earth Spirit is saying.

Thus, we see how people in this age of the development of the consciousness soul have to struggle for an awareness of the world. We have to understand these things with our emotions so that we will approach the anthroposophical world view with our feelings, with our heart's blood, so to speak. It is this world view and not just isolated ideas about the world that modern people need to adopt if they want to understand themselves with the right feelings and thoughts according to my indications here.

February 10, 1923

EARTHLY LEARNING AND HEAVENLY WISDOM: HUMAN BEINGS AS CITIZENS OF THE UNIVERSE AND HERMITS ON THE EARTH

PART II

THE GREAT change in the spiritual development of humanity that took place in recent centuries and that I have described from many different perspectives has not only changed the intellectual and theoretical character of cognition and perception but has also affected the feelings and emotions in the human soul and therefore all of human life. To fully realize this, we will look today at the actual foundations of life, that is, not only at various more or less pronounced symptoms of this change, but also at life's characteristic forms of expression where we will be able to trace this shift in human consciousness.

We have often talked about the centers of learning in ancient times of human evolution, namely, the Mystery centers. These Mystery centers were, so to speak, completely clothed in human veneration. People spoke of the Mysteries as being the most important thing on earth for humanity. Everything significant and meaningful for human life was believed to radiate from them. Basically, people then believed that if there were no Mysteries among them, they could not be what the gods had intended them to be. Indeed, people looked with the greatest reverence and the deepest respect to the Mysteries. They felt gratitude for the Mysteries because they realized what they received from the Mysteries allowed them to become on earth what the gods had wanted human beings to be.

When we compare this with people's attitudes toward educational institutions nowadays, we will find nothing like that deep and warm reverence anywhere. In fact, we will often find that when people have completed their compulsory education, they feel a great sense of relief and are happy to be done with it. But even aside from this extreme, we know that educational institutions do not really give us what we regard as essential for our humanness, for being truly human. Even though we may venerate with a kind of theoretical reverence what we learn in chemistry laboratories, biology institutes, law schools, and in schools of philosophy, we will still not feel that the existence of such institutions gives us an awareness of our true humanity.

Thus, we cannot claim that people everywhere are directing their warmest feelings of reverence to these educational institutions even though they may have a certain kind of theoretical feeling for them. At any rate, nowadays it will not happen often that university students working on a paper for a seminar will feel themselves permeated by their whole elemental humanness the way a Mystery pupil did in ancient times when he or she had completed one of the stages of the training.

Yet, we need to be connected with something we can deeply venerate, something from which we feel the divine streaming out. Let us compare this cultural-historical fact with its origins, and go back two or three millennia before the Mystery of Golgotha when centers of learning similar to the Mysteries existed in the Near East. In these centers, people studied above all the natural sciences of their time, if we can call them that. They studied the starry heavens, the nature of the stars, their movements, their rhythmical appearance at certain times, and so on. People nowadays imagine that these studies in astronomy may even have had an element of fantasy. However, that is not how it was. These studies were carried out with the same, if not greater, methodical thoroughness and care as mineralogy, geology, or biology are these days.

What did people in ancient times think when they studied the starry heavens? They believed that if they could understand the starry heavens, they would know something about the nature and destiny of human beings on earth. Their studies in astronomy culminated in insights into the fate of human beings and whole peoples on earth based on the constellations in the sky.

They looked at the stars not merely with theoretical intentions and ideas. Rather they did so out of the awareness that if they knew the relationship of Saturn to the sun or to a sign of the zodiac at the moment when a person is born or has accomplished a great deed, then they would know how the heavens have placed human beings on the earth. They would know to what extent human beings are the creations, the children, of the heavens. They studied the heavens in order to understand what could be a guideline for their life on earth. All the insights they gathered in their astronomy were geared to understanding human beings. All their knowledge was warmed through and through by a truly human element. And people in those days believed what they were doing was connected to what they could study in the heavens.

We can look at an example from the realm of human artistic activity. In those ancient times, when people began writing poetry or composing music, they drew their inspiration from the heavens. I have often mentioned that Homer did not write the line "Of Peleus's son, Achilles, sing, O Muse, the vengeance deep and deadly; ..." just to use a nice poetic phrase. He used it because he knew he was expressing something that did not spring from his human poetic craft; he was expressing what the heavens were whispering to him. Those who made music on earth were reproducing through the sound of earthly instruments what they believed they heard in the music of the heavenly spheres. People felt that in the way they worked, related to other people, and formed communities here on earth they experienced the will impulses that streamed down upon them from the universe. They studied these will impulses in their observation of the starry heavens and felt that they were acting here on earth in accordance with the intentions of the heavens.

In other words, all the science, art, and religion of these ancient times flowed into human life and work. For in those days religion, science, and art were united; they were a unity that ultimately radiated into human beings so they could feel themselves as the beings the gods had wanted them to be on earth. This attitude prevailed as long as people found a spiritual element in their knowledge about the heavens—as long as they were open to perceive something spiritual in the nature and movements of the stars and in their rhythmic appearance. They perceived a spiritual element that streamed down to them through what they knew about the stars so that they could put their knowledge into practice on earth.

Astrology does not have a good name these days. However, when we think of it in the old sense, it has a more respectable name. People back then looked up to the stars, and that is where the Logos revealed itself to them. It worked through their thoughts, their imagination, and their language here on earth. People participated in what made the formation of sounds here on earth resound with the mysteries of the heavens by merely setting their speech organs into motion. The Logos, which is the intelligence ruling in the human race, appeared as an emanation of the world of the stars. People believed what happened down here on earth was a reflection of the archetypal picture they knew through their astrology.

When we look at our modern knowledge, we realize that it has been gained through sensory observation of earthly things. Even our modern astronomy, as I explained yesterday, is only earthly knowledge projected onto the heavens. Human beings nowadays are gaining knowledge based on their senses, and, indeed, they are integrated into the world differently than they were in the past. I described this difference recently in the course of these lectures. As I explained in my book, *The Philosophy of Freedom*, modern intellectual people are characterized by their abstract concepts and their freedom, which has become possible only because of the development of abstract and intellectual concepts that are not in any way compelling, but provide moral commandments originating in human individuality.[1] These intellectual concepts and the consciousness of freedom are a relatively recent development in human evolution. They appeared after the consciousness based on astrology had vanished—the consciousness that saw human beings as creatures that carry out the intentions of the gods. We modern human beings with our intellect and our freedom are cut off from the heavens; we have truly become earth hermits and rely completely on the earth for all our knowledge. The way we gain knowledge explains why we have such a strong interest in and attachment to it.

In ancient times it would have been unthinkable to see religion and scientific knowledge as two different things. When people in those days arrived at a scientific insight, it immediately also gave them a religious feeling, showing them the way to the gods. In fact, they could not help being religious in the true sense of the word once they had gained knowledge. Nowadays people can learn the whole spectrum of current knowledge, and yet it will not make them religious. I would like to know whether anyone has become religious these days through having become a botanist, zoologist, or chemist!

People who want to be religious look for religion in addition to knowledge. That is why we have separate institutions for the cultivation of religious life besides those for learning and knowledge. In fact, many people think that knowledge diverts us from the path of religion and that, therefore, we must look for other ways to lead us back to religion. Nevertheless, in our lectures we have had to stress again and again the importance of modern knowledge. We have had to point out that recent insights and findings are indeed essential for modern humanity and its further development.

Modern human beings with their intellectualism and consciousness of freedom develop here on earth what people in ancient times, who still had a heavenly consciousness, developed only after death. In describing what happens to modern people immediately after death, we have to point

out that they look back upon a picture of their life by dis-
carding their etheric body. Then, in the period after that,
they wander back through their life from the ending to the
beginning. In ancient times, life after death was different.
What people could see on earth only through higher revelation, namely, an intellectual world view, they did not get
until after death. What they were to gain on earth could be
present there only as an ideal; they would be free human
beings only after death. In those times, the true human being appeared only after the crossing from the physical world
into the spiritual one.

In other words, what people in ancient times experienced
only after death in looking back on their earthly life, namely
intellectualism and a consciousness of freedom, modern
people have crammed already into their life between birth
and death. They have become intellectual beings endowed
with a consciousness of freedom while still on earth.

However, in the process we have to gain something
through our sensory knowledge and our inferences based
on it that does not much interest us at first. No matter how
long we observe the world of the stars through our tele-
scopes, it will not make us feel humanly and inwardly
warmed and enlightened. Expeditions of astronomers and
natural scientists are fitted out to verify Einstein's ideas.[2]
But nobody expects his or her findings to be something that
belongs so intimately to our elemental human nature as did
those of the astronomers in the Babylonian or Assyrian culture. What our modern knowledge gives us is very different:
a lack of interest in the vast reaches of the universe. Though
this or that recent biological discovery may be very interesting, we cannot say that through these biological discoveries
people come closer to the divine-spiritual being they carry

in their soul. Instead, people want to approach this divine-spiritual being in their soul through a separate interest in religion.

These days people do not have any clear idea of the relationship the ancients had to knowledge, even in the not so distant past. We need only think of what a fateful experience it was when Archimedes discovered the Archimedean principle while he was in the bathtub and exclaimed the fateful words: "I have found it!" A single insight such as this one was like a window allowing a glimpse into the secrets of the universe.

Such a warmhearted attitude toward knowledge certainly did not exist when X rays were discovered.[3] We could say that the modern relationship to knowledge leads more to an open-mouthed gasping with surprise than to an inward rejoicing in the soul. From a human point of view these two gestures and attitudes are very different, and this difference has to be considered in terms of humanity's further development.

All this has led to a very strange development. For several centuries now, people have been receiving in their earthly life what they received only after death in ancient times, namely, intellectual understanding of the world and a consciousness of freedom. Yet, they have hardly noticed this; their world of feelings, the elemental part of their world, has hardly been touched. In fact, we could say that all this is more likely to have a bitter taste for people. After all, they do not consider pure thoughts the way I have tried to do in *The Philosophy of Freedom*, that is, they do not respond by wanting to sing hymns to them rather than analyze them. Consciousness of freedom has led people into all kinds of tumultuous things, but not to the realization that something has descended from heaven to the earth. Thus, not even the basic force underlying the modern development of humanity has been felt on a purely human level.

To explain why this is so is to answer one of the most important questions of human existence. In ancient times people gained knowledge by looking up to the heavens to find the Logos there. They looked for what the gods were telling them through the movements and the nature of the stars; their human intelligence was a reflection of the divine Logos. Everything people did on earth was illuminated by the content of the Logos, and this content had been received from the stars. In those days, human life would have been nothing if people could not have given it meaning on the basis of their knowledge of the world of the stars.

Similarly, all the knowledge we gain inwardly is in a sense a mere nothing. We get this knowledge by submitting ourselves to the study of botany, zoology, biology, physiology, or other subjects. We do all this out of ambition, at best, or based on the insight that it is necessary if we want to eke out a living here on earth. I know this is a radical statement, but in a sense it comes close to the truth. For surely the people who see great ideals here are under the influence of a certain illusion that allows them to interpret these things in accordance with their ideals. In any case, the people who can see meaning in the sentence "I pray a chemical formula" are few and far between. This is how we have to express an important cultural-historical fact, albeit a negative one.

It takes a person such as Novalis, who was gifted with a profound knowledge aglow with youthful enthusiasm, to feel that, for example, solving a differential equation is actually praying.[4] Ordinary mathematicians are not in a very prayerful mood when they discover the solution to a differential equation. The obvious fact that we are involved with our whole being in the act of knowing, that we feel our longing for the divine with our whole being, is not at all self-evident to modern humanity. But people take it as a matter of course that those who climb to the heights of knowledge are glad when they have their exams behind them and do not have to go through any more. The joy of having passed through the stages of the Mysteries is hardly to be found in modern exam candidates. At least it is extremely rare nowadays that students talk with the full seriousness of the ancient Mysteries about the profoundly divine deed a professor has done in giving them a dissertation topic and enabling them to go through the waters of holiness while they work on their topic. Yet that would be the normal, the self-evident thing to do.

Keeping this in mind, let me sketch it for you. We have down here the earth with everything on it (see drawing p. 64, white and green). In ancient times, those who were seeking knowledge saw all these things, but they believed that they could only fully understand them when they looked up to the stars and received from there the rays that illuminated everything for them in the right way (see drawing, red).

In ancient times, seekers looked for this reflection of the world of the stars in earthly life (see drawing, lower red). Without this reflection, everything I have drawn down here in outline would have seemed worthless to them. Nowadays we do not concern ourselves with what is up there, but study only what is here below. We study it in innumerable details, and when we have devoted ourselves to this or that specialized discipline, our head is filled with many details. However, evaluating and weighing these details has become a matter of indifference in our life, and consequently we also

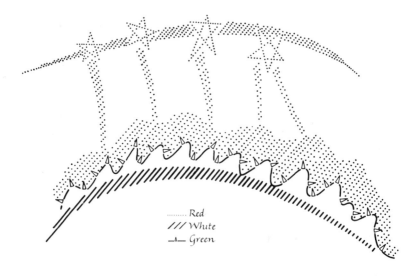

.... Red
/// White
—ı— Green

lack interest for the noble primordial human element in us. This has an especially striking impact on our spirituality as such.

The Swabian writer Friedrich Theodor Vischer poked fun at the fact that what we must leave behind in order to reach knowledge does not matter anymore to the consciousness of humanity as a whole.[5] He claimed that one of the most "significant" treatises in the field of modern literature is the one on the connection between the chilblains of Frau Christiane von Goethe and the symbolical-allegorical figures in Part Two of *Faust*! Why shouldn't a dissertation be written about this connection just as well as about any other subject? After all, the method used and the human interest involved would not be of any different quality than in cases where somebody writes a treatise—as does indeed happen— on the dashes in Homer's poetry. Truly, we are proud of accumulating insights people in ancient times considered worthwhile only after they had been illuminated by knowledge of the heavens.

We do not have heavenly wisdom. We do not study copper by looking at Venus or lead by looking at Saturn. We also do not study primeval human beings by looking at the sign of Aquarius, and we do not understand what moves from the animal nature of the lion to certain inner impulses of human nature by studying the sign of Leo. We no longer draw anything down from the heavens to help us explain earthly things; instead, we turn our gaze solely on the vast number of details all over the earth.

Clearly, then, we need something that brings meaning into the separate details and helps us to see once again what people used to see when they beheld earthly objects illumined by the heavens. We know many things, but we need a comprehensive knowledge that can radiate into all the separate fields of knowledge and give them meaning. That is what anthroposophy wants to be.

Just as astrology looked into the heavens to explain the earth, so anthroposophy wants to look within human beings to see what they have to say out of themselves. From there it wants to illuminate everything we know about minerals, plants, animals, human beings, and everything else we usually know only in separate details. Just as people looked to the heavens to understand earthly life, so we with our intellect and our newly acquired freedom must now come to understand ourselves. Only then will we be able to look again at the moment of death when we enter a spiritual world where gods will gaze down upon what we will bring with us and what will radiate from us. For we are to become fully human already on earth, whereas in ancient times this did not happen until after death. How far we have been successful in becoming truly human will be evident from the strength we gain from the pure awareness of our humanity. We receive this pure consciousness of our humanity through what radiates from anthroposophy into everything we can know and accomplish on earth.

"In the beginning was the Word, and the Word was with God, and the Word was God," (John 1:1) that is to say, in the beginning was the Logos and the Logos was with God, and the Logos was God. The Logos was brought down from the revelation of the gods in the heavens. "And the Word became flesh and dwelt among us," (John 1:14) and, indeed, it continues to live among us. The Logos has become flesh. What could once be found only in the heavens must now be sought in the human realm. In ancient times, people were right in seeing the Logos with God the Father, but in our time it has to be sought in the realm of God the Son.

We find God the Son in his basic significance when we understand St. Paul's words "I have been crucified with Christ; it is no longer I who live, but Christ who lives in me," (Gal. 2:20) that is, when we come to know ourselves. All of anthroposophy aims at penetrating into our very depths. What did people in ancient times find when they looked into their depths? They found luciferic forces at the heart of human nature. When modern people penetrate deeply enough into their own being, they find Christ. That is the other side of the change from ancient to modern times. Since intellectualism and the consciousness of freedom came down from the heavens to the earth and since Christ united himself with humanity on earth, human beings can find Christ in the depths of their own being if they penetrate deeply enough. In contrast, when people in ancient times penetrated deeply into themselves, they found luciferic spirits.

That is what the candidates of the ancient Mysteries were supposed to learn. They had to realize that when they penetrated deep down into human nature, they would ultimately find at the heart of their own soul something that would make them recoil in horror, namely, the luciferic forces. Therefore, they had to learn to look up to the moment of death, for they would become truly human only after passing through the portal of death. Then they would be rescued from the luciferic forces they found here on earth in the depths of their soul. That is what the death experience in the ancient Mysteries was about. That is why the Mystery pupils in ancient times had to concentrate on learning about and picturing the moment of death.

In our times, we have to take hold of what has been given to us: intellectualism and consciousness of freedom. If we take hold of them in the right way, by permeating all our earthly knowledge and our actions with what pours forth out of a pure consciousness of humanity such as anthroposophy strives for, then we find the Christ forces in the depths of our soul. We will then realize that while people looked to the constellations of the stars in ancient times to understand human destiny on earth, we must now look to the human being. In this way we learn how the human being, permeated by the Christ substance here on earth while possessing full humanness, then lights up for the universe. The human being lights up as the star of humanity after having gone through the portal of death.

This is the spiritual humanism that can take the place of ancient astrology. It can teach us to consider what is revealed in us as Sophia, namely, anthroposophia, as people did the revelation of the stars as Logia in ancient times. That is the awareness with which we must permeate ourselves. That is how we can come to know the cosmic significance of the human being. We will understand our cosmic significance that leads us to study first the physical body and then the body of formative forces or etheric body.

I want to mention here only one example. When we study our physical body in the right way, that is, by illuminating this body with anthroposophy, we will learn that it is subject to its own forces. When our body subjects itself to its own forces, it continuously tends to become ill. Indeed, our lower part, our physical body, always has a tendency to become ill. And when we then study the etheric body, we find there the totality of the forces that constantly work to make the sick human being well again. The pendulum swings between physical body and etheric body aiming to keep the balance between the pathological and the therapeutical. In other words, our etheric body is the cosmic therapist, and our physical body the cosmic pathogenic agent.

We can say the same about other areas of human knowledge. We have to ask ourselves what we have to do when we are confronted with an illness. Well, we have to manage somehow, through some combination of remedies, to call upon the etheric body for healing. Basically, this is what all of medicine is doing: it somehow calls upon the patient's etheric body for healing. We are on the right path toward healing a patient who can be cured when we appeal to his or her etheric body in the right way, that is, when we seek the healing forces that can flow into the patient from his or her etheric body in accordance with the individual's destiny.

But I will say more about this tomorrow, when I want to speak in more detail about this last aspect of today's topic.

LECTURE SIX

February 11, 1923

THE INVISIBLE HUMAN BEING
WITHIN US

WE CAN clearly distinguish two entities in human beings. As you may remember, I have recently explained in several lectures that our physical organism is spiritually prepared in the life before birth. It is then sent down, so to speak, as spiritual organization before we actually enter earthly life with our I. Basically, this spiritual organization continues to work throughout our physical life on earth, but it does not manifest in outer, visible form. Its visible parts—the sheaths enclosing the fetus during the gestation period: chorion, amnion, allantois—are discarded at birth. Nevertheless, this pre-earthly organization continues to be active within us throughout our whole life. Yet, it is of a different nature than our physical-soul-spiritual being during our life on earth, and that is what I would like to talk about today.

In a sense, we have an invisible human being in us living in our growth forces, in the hidden forces working in nutrition, and, in fact, in all the realms that are outside the control of our conscious activity. The influence of this invisible human being extends to this unconscious activity, into our growth and even the daily restoration of our forces through nutrition. These influences are the aftereffects of our pre-earthly existence, which becomes a body of forces during life on earth that works in us without our being aware of it. Today I want to describe in more detail the nature and organization of this invisible human being we all carry in us in our forces of growth, nutrition, and reproduction.

We can approach this by means of a diagram that shows that this invisible being also has an I, an astral organization, an etheric organization or body of formative forces, and a physical organization. Of course, after our birth, its physical organization rests inside our other physical organism. In the course of today's lecture, you will understand how this invisible human being affects our physical organization. Thus,

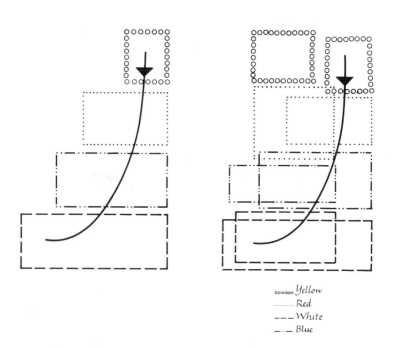

oooooo Yellow

.... Red

——— White

—..— Blue

to represent all this diagrammatically, I have to draw it like this (see drawing, left side):

First of all, this invisible human being has its I-organization (yellow), then its astral organization (red), its etheric organization (blue), and finally its physical organism (white). This physical organism of the invisible human being affects only our processes of growth and nutrition, in short, everything in the lower human being, the metabolic-limb system as we have described it. All the streams of forces in this invisible being proceed from the I-organization and flow through the astral and etheric organizations into the physical one, where they then spread out (see arrow in left drawing, p. 70).

In the embryonal phase, this physical organization is in the sheaths or membranes enclosing the embryo. After we are born, this physical organization of the invisible being is contained in our processes of nutrition and restoration. Outwardly, the physical organization we are speaking of here is thus not separate from our physical organism; rather the two are united (see right drawing, p. 70).

In addition to this invisible human being in us, there is our visible being after we are born. I will draw this visible human being beside the invisible one. Here you see what the interpenetration of the physical and supra-physical during life on earth looks like. During our earthly life, there is a constant stream flowing from our I through the astral and etheric bodies into our physical body (see arrow in drawing on the right). After we are born, this stream takes its course in the metabolic-limb system, in the forces of outer movement and those of inner movement that transport the food we have taken in through our whole organism and even up into the brain.

There is also a direct intervention, a working of forces

that proceeds from the I directly into the whole human being (see p. 88, Illustration 1). In other words, there is the
influence of an activity, a stream as it were, that enters from
the I directly into the nerve-sense system, bypassing the astral
and etheric bodies, and acting directly on our physical body.
Of course, this force is strongest in the head where most of
the sense organs are concentrated, but it does extend over
the whole human being, for example, through the sense of
touch in the skin. By the same token, I would also have to
draw a stream for the taking in of food through the mouth.
Thus, in our head there is an organization that streams up
from below; it starts from the I and passes through the astral
and etheric bodies, through the physical body, and then streams
up into the I. In addition, there is another stream flowing
directly into the physical body and streaming downward.

The nerve tract is the visible sign of this direct stream
that flows from the I into our physical organism (see p. 88,
Illustration 1, yellow). The I-organization, then, runs alongside the nerve tracts. Basically, this I-organization has a destructive influence on the organism for here spirit directly
enters into physical matter, and where this happens we find
a process of destruction. In other words, alongside the nerve
tracts and coming from the senses, there is a subtle process
of death spreading throughout our organism.

We can trace the stream that flows in the invisible human
being into the astral, etheric, and physical bodies when we
track our blood vessels all the way into the sense organs (see
p. 88, Illustration 1, red). Thus, we find that the I flows in
the blood in such a way that its forces have first been ensouled by the astral, the etheric, and the physical organizations. Taking the astral and etheric organizations with it,
the I streams upward through the physical organization in
our blood.

In other words, the whole invisible human being flows in the blood process as an anabolic or growth process that continually regenerates us through the assimilation of nutrients. In terms of our diagram, this stream flows upward, pours itself into the sense organs, including the skin, and then meets the other stream that enters from the I directly into the physical organism. Of course, in reality all this is even more complicated because we would also have to consider our breathing process.

In the breathing process the I indeed flows into the astral body and from there directly into the lungs by means of air. Thus, the supersensible human being is also the foundation of our breathing processes. However, here, unlike in the nerve-sense system, the I does not intervene directly in the physical organism; instead, the I saturates itself with astral forces, takes up oxygen, and only then does it enter the organism with the help of the breathing process (see p. 88, Illustration 1, third arrow). Of course, now we are no longer dealing with a pure I-organization but with an I-astral organization. We could say, then, that the breathing process is a diminished death process.

The nerve-sense process is the actual process of death; the breathing process, on the other hand, is a weakened death process. It is countered by the process where the I is strengthened by streaming first into the etheric body and it is only taken up by the physical body (see p. 88, Illustration 1, fourth arrow). This process, however, runs its course mostly in the supersensible realm and therefore cannot be traced by ordinary physiology. Its outward effect is the pulse beat. This process is also a regenerative one, although not as much as the actual metabolic regeneration processes; it is only a weakened regenerative process. It meets up with the breathing process. To a certain extent, the breathing process is a destructive process. If we took in more oxygen, our life would be much shorter. Our life is lengthened to the extent the intake of oxygen is compensated for by carbon dioxide formation in the blood.

Thus, everything in the organism works closely together, and only if we resort to the supersensible human being can we fully understand what is happening in our body. Although after birth this supersensible being has only an invisible form, we are aware of these forces precisely on the basis of the anthroposophical understanding of the human being.

For instance, when we examine our eyes on this basis, we find that the blood process with its delicate ramifications (see p. 88, Illustration 2, red) is taken up by the nerve process (yellow) that runs in the opposite direction. The blood process always runs its course toward the periphery; it is centrifugal. The nerve process, which is really a process of breakdown, always runs centripetally, that is, from the periphery toward the center. All other processes in our body are metamorphoses of these two.

If the process going on between our pulse and breathing takes its course as it should, then the lower human being is connected with the upper one in the right way. Then we are healthy, at least inwardly and if we have not received external injuries. Destructive processes spread in the organism only when breakdown or catabolism predominates. We become ill when foreign elements accumulate in our organism, elements that are not assimilated in the right way and contain too many catabolic forces, that is, too much that is akin to the physical nature of our environment.

The pathological processes that result in foreign formations are caused by the direct intervention of the spiritual by way of the I. These foreign formations may not be readily visible as physical accumulations of matter; for example, they may be in the fluid or even in the aeriform human being. Nevertheless, they are foreign elements in the human body. As they develop, they will not meet up with a healthy process streaming up from below alongside the blood vessels. As a result, the foreign elements, which have the tendency to proliferate into tumors and then to crumble, cannot be dissolved. Of course, if the blood-building process meets up with them in the right way, these foreign elements are dissolved and assimilated into our organism's life processes. However, if there is an obstruction because an excessively strong catabolic process works downward, that catabolic process takes hold of one or the other organ. Then foreign bodies form within us; at first they are like an exudate or a tumor, but they have the tendency to take the same course as those outer processes of earthly nature that crumble. Here, it is important to realize that we have not sufficiently integrated the invisible human being I have drawn here next to the physical one into ourselves.

Actually we cannot really speak here of healing by human means. In reality, this is how it is: As soon as too much centripetal activity occurs in connection with the nerve-sense system—that is, too much of the processes in our outer environment are crammed into us and thus cause tumors somewhere in us that later break to pieces—the other system that runs its course alongside the blood vessels rebels and wants to bring about healing. It wants to permeate what is in the organism with the right astral and etheric force that can stream up from below, and it wants to keep the I or the astral body and the I from working by themselves. The healer then has to assist this revolutionary principle in our organism. Healing is actually nothing else than supporting the organism's own healing forces from the outside.

Thus, the appearance of a tumor is a symptom indicating that the I-activity is not working properly out of the etheric body. It makes itself felt, but sometimes it cannot get at the tumor. In a sense, we have to assist the etheric body in this direction so that it can become active. We can support the healing process in our organism by helping the etheric body to be active in the right way. In other words, it must first be permeated by the I and the astral body and then get at what is coming from above and has not yet taken in the etheric influence, but is imbued only with influences from the I and the astral body.

In this way, we can counter the poisonous effects of the I and the astral body on our organism with the etheric influences. All we really need to know is through what remedies the etheric organization, properly permeated by the astral and I-organization, will have to intervene in the organism in such a case. The remedies are needed only to assist the etheric organization, as it were. Thus, we have to know what remedies will strengthen the etheric organization so it can pit its anabolic forces against the excessive catabolic forces. You see, the pathology on which any therapy is based cannot be understood at all without resorting to the invisible human being.

However, it is also possible that our I-organization and astral body—in other words, our soul-spiritual organization—do not enter properly into the physical organization. In a sense, then, our soul-spiritual organization may not have pushed through far enough into our physical one. If that is the case, we will always suffer from a predominance of what works upward as growth forces and did not get sufficient weight or gravity through its integration into the physical organization. In other words, people may be born with a condition where their invisible human being does not sufficiently take hold of their physical body.

For example, the invisible human being I have sketched here may refuse, so to speak, to work appropriately in the blood process. In that case, the spirit does not have access to the blood process, and as a result the individuals in question are often pale already in their childhood and remain skinny, or sometimes they shoot up quickly because of the predominating growth forces. That is what happens when the soul-spiritual element cannot enter the organism in the right way. And because the body here refuses to allow the soul-spiritual in, we must effect a weakening of the overly strong activity in the etheric body. In the case of pale, skinny, and gaunt children, we must work to reduce the etheric body's hypertrophic, overly active forces to their proper level. We must see to it that these children get more gravity or weight into their body; for instance, the blood will have the proper weight when it receives the necessary amount of iron. As a consequence the etheric body will work less strongly upward; its upward effect will be weakened.

Another symptom of this condition is that in such people the night processes, as I would like to call them, predominate over the day processes. During the night, when we sleep, the physical-etheric organization refuses to take in the spiritual-soul organization. Our night organization when we lie asleep in our beds—not that of the invisible human being who is outside us at night—is overly strong in people who have the kind of congenital consumption I have just described. We therefore have to support and strengthen the day organization, that is, we have to give it a certain weight by boosting the catabolic processes. For it is by fostering the catabolic processes that lead to an inner hardening and ultimately to a crumbling or breaking down—of course, this should happen only to a very minimal extent during the cure—that we can push back the over-flowing forces of the etheric body and hold the consumption in check.

Thus, our knowledge of the whole human being makes this interaction between health and illness—which is essentially balanced through the relationship between pulse and breathing—transparent to us. When we learn how we can foster this or that through outer remedies, then we are able to support the natural healing processes that are always there but do not always manifest themselves.

After all, we cannot introduce a completely foreign process into our organism. What always happens is that when we bring any foreign process into our body, the former is at once inwardly transformed into its opposite. For example, the food you eat contains certain chemical forces. As the organism takes these in, it transforms them right away into their opposites. This has to be possible, for if our food keeps its outer character for too long after we have eaten it, it gets to our catabolism and causes destructive, deadly catabolic processes. What enters our body with our food must be taken up right away by inner processes and be changed into its opposite.

You can trace the processes I have just described on the basis of the human being as a whole in many details. For example, let us assume that somehow a splinter of something or other entered your body (see p. 88, Illustration 3, yellow). Now, your body can react to this foreign object in one of two ways. First, let's assume you cannot pull it out and it stays within you. The anabolic forces in the blood-stream are active all around the foreign object within you (see p. 88, Illustration 3, red). They gather around the "intruder" and have thus moved from their proper place. As a result, the nerve activity right away predominates. A kind of exudate is secreted around the foreign body (blue), and the intruder is encapsulated. Because of this cyst formation the following happens. If we had no foreign element at this place, the etheric body would act in a certain way on the physical body there. Now, however, the etheric body cannot intervene in the foreign element; rather, a cyst develops that is completely filled with the etheric (red lines). Thus, a part of our body contains a foreign element; in this part our etheric body is not structured by the physical.

In such cases it is then a matter of strengthening the astral body to such an extent that it can work on this piece of etheric body without the help of the physical body. Through the encapsulation, our body has called upon the catabolic forces to isolate them in a particular part of the body and to integrate the healing etheric body in that place. The etheric body then has to be supported through proper treatment by the astral and the I.

In a sense, in such a case what is above the physical in us has to become so strong that it can work without the physical in one small part of our organism. This is what always happens when a splinter or some other foreign element is encysted as part of the healing process. In that part of our body, we are moved up one level, as it were, with our whole organization. Of course, it is also possible that a foreign body is formed within our own organism, and the same applies there.

However, it is also possible that a completely different process runs its course when we have a splinter in our body. It can happen that the nerve activity around the splinter increases and predominates over the blood activity (see p.

89, Illustration 4, yellow). This nerve activity, in which the I reinforced by the astral body is at work, then stimulates the blood activity and prevents the coagulation of the exudate. Instead, it agitates the secretions and ultimately leads to the formation of pus (white). Since the nerves push through to the outside (see arrows), the pus is also pushed to the outside through the thrust that runs along the nerve tracts in the catabolic activities toward the periphery. Thus, the pus runs outside the body and the splinter is discharged with it. A scar then forms, and the wound heals.

As you can see from the processes of encystation, which occur especially when the splinter is too deep inside our organism for the nerve-sense system to push it out, the anabolic forces of the blood will predominate and lead to encapsulation. If the splinter is closer to the body surface, then the thrust from the nerves, the catabolic forces, will be stronger and stimulate the substance that then becomes the exudate. They will use the already existing paths of catabolism for this purpose of breakdown, and the whole thing will suppurate.

Thus, in the beginning of this process, in the moment of originating, so to speak, we always carry within us the latent tendency to let our organism harden toward the center, centripetally, and to dissolve it again toward the periphery, centrifugally. Of course, in the normal course of events in our organism, the inward process of tumor formation and the outward one of inflammation and pus formation are in equilibrium. Our inflammations are usually so strong that we can overcome the catabolic force of tumor formation. It is only when one or the other of these forces predominates that we develop either a real tumor or a severe inflammation.

Now, don't think that all this works out as easily and

simply in reality as we necessarily have to present it in a schematic description. In reality, these processes are meshed. For example, you know that when the inflammatory forces are strong, we also often have a fever. Basically, this is caused by overly strong, excessive anabolic processes in the blood. Indeed, the forces we often develop during a fever would almost be sufficient to supply energy for another person if they could be conducted there.

On the other hand, when the catabolic forces predominate, we have cold symptoms, which are not as easy to diagnose as a fever. Of course, sometimes the two conditions alternate, and so, in practice, we often have to deal with an intermingling of what we really need to keep separate to fully understand the matter.

Concerning the poisons in nature, such as that in the deadly nightshade or belladonna, we have to ask how these poisons relate to the other substances in our environment that are edible and not poisonous. With our food we take into our organism what is formed outside in nature in a similar way as our invisible human being—it starts from a spiritual process (see p. 89, Illustration 5, yellow), enters an astral process (red), then an etheric one (blue), and finally a physical one (white). The activity that proceeds downward in nature, from the periphery down onto the earth, is akin to the inner activity of our I, which is purely spiritual. This activity, which I have here drawn yellow, flows down but is transformed on the way from the astral and then is changed again on the way from the etheric, and then enters into the physical, and is finally absorbed by plants. Plants grow toward and absorb this etheric activity, which from further up already brings with it the astral and the I processes, that is, the soul and the spiritual processes.

However, it is different with the poisonous substances.

Unlike the ordinary green plant substances, the poisonous substances typically do not turn toward the etheric. Instead, they go directly to the astral. In other words, the astral, which I have drawn red, enters this substance (see p. 00, Illustration 5, red in white). In the case of the deadly nightshade, the fruit becomes extremely greedy and is not satisfied with taking in the etheric, but it also directly assimilates the astral before the latter has absorbed the life forces through the etheric on its way down. We could say astral substance is constantly trickling down onto the earth without having entered the etheric realm first. Drops of this astral substance that have not gone through the earth's etheric atmosphere can be found in the poison of the deadly nightshade. The poisons in the thorn apple and hyoscyamine, which is found in henbane, are also drops of the cosmic astral that has trickled down.

Consequently, what lives in such plant substances, for example, in the belladonna or deadly nightshade, is akin to the process that enters our nerves and oxygen circulation directly from the I or the astral body. Thus, when we ingest the poison of the deadly nightshade, our catabolic processes, which usually enter our physical body directly from the I, will be greatly enhanced. Our I is not strong enough to bear such an increase. If the counteracting force that works from below upward in the blood circulation is too strong, then we can oppose it with such catabolic processes; then the poison of the deadly nightshade, atropin, can be an antidote to excessive growth processes if it is given in small doses. Of course, if we take too much of this poison, we can no longer speak about establishing a balance. In case of an overdose, first the growth processes are suppressed, and the patient becomes befuddled by a spiritual activity that his or her I cannot yet tolerate. Indeed, our I may be able to stand this activity only in future stages of being, such as the Venus or Vulcan stage. And then the typical symptoms of poisoning appear. First, the point of origin of the activity at work in the blood is undermined. This is followed by the gastric symptoms that are the first stages of deadly nightshade poisoning. The forces working upward are prevented from functioning normally and complete unconsciousness and the destruction of the person by catabolic processes set in.

You see, if we know the spiritual content of a substance we take in—and we can study all this best in plants—we can trace exactly how the substance will work in our organism. Of course, we must combine this with accurate knowledge of outer nature. We have to know what lives in each plant, and then we will also know how each plant works and how it affects us when we eat it. This knowledge will lead to great achievements if we can also bring about social conditions that allow us to put these insights into practice.

Nowadays, however, even when we have the knowledge, we are usually not able to practice it because our social conditions are not adapted to an understanding of nature. Nature is studied as a separate entity and in abstraction only. Therefore, people cannot understand how we are incorporated into the universe. For the same reason, it is not possible to arrange things on a large scale so that we can say, for example, this or that person needs to be given this or that plant substance in such and such a rhythm. To make this possible to any great extent, our scientific medicine will have to take on a different character. In other words, our social institutions must be connected to what we know about our relationship to nature.

Of course, a great deal can be done in individual cases. For example, we can boil roots and make a decoction for a person whose catabolic processes, which start in the head, we know to be excessive. We use certain roots because we know they contain substances that have drawn—by virtue of being in a root—the spiritual, soul, and etheric elements down into the physical root formation in the right way. These substances of root formation can then work in our organism all the way into the peripheral blood vessels and into our head; they can then be called upon to counteract the excessive catabolic process of the nervous system. Of course, we must have a clear idea of the transformations a root substance undergoes when it is taken in through our mouth and is then digested so that it can reach the outermost periphery of our head organization and skin organization.

In other cases, we will have to know how substances taken from blossoms work, that is, substances whose connection with the etheric is already somewhat loose and shaky. Such blossom substances strongly absorb the astral element and are a little bit like poisons. They can be added to the bath water and thus enter the organism in an entirely different way. They stimulate the weak anabolism in the blood vessels and counteract the catabolism working toward the periphery.

Similarly, we can also trace the effect of injections. Basically, this is also a matter of strengthening and enhancing anabolic processes to counterbalance the catabolic processes. Therefore, we will see the reactions of the catabolic processes especially when we give injections. In fact, injections have their proper effect only when the catabolic processes resist at first before gradually merging with the anabolic processes. Thus, slightly impaired vision or a buzzing in the ears often occurs with injections because the breakdown processes at first refuse to properly counterbalance the enhanced anabolic processes. By the same token, such reactions are a definite indication that we are intervening in these processes.

All this shows you that anthroposophy is not about providing models for a club of sectarian old cronies so they can expound on the human being consisting of physical body, etheric body, astral body, and I. Rather, anthroposophy is concerned with a serious, thorough understanding of human beings and their relationship to the world; it is a matter of carrying the spiritual into the material realm. If anthroposophy is to take its rightful place in the world, people must realize that it can observe and study the spiritual in the material realm. As long as we are only working for sectarian circles, who merely pass on their classification of human beings, we are only dealing with things that will conflict with all kinds of other sectarian ideas. However, as soon as we can actually show that our anthroposophical insights are closely connected with all other knowledge—as I said yesterday, they shed light on all other earthly knowledge just as astrology did in the past—then people will realize that anthroposophy has to intervene in the process of civilization so that a true upbuilding process can occur to counterbalance the breakdown processes coming from past ages.

This is how serious we have to be about professing ourselves anthroposophists. Of course, not every individual will do research to discover how belladonna on the one hand and chlorine on the other affect our organism. That is not the point; what matters is that people generally understand in their hearts and minds that we can receive healing precisely from anthroposophical insights into the world and the human being.

Similarly, in Waldorf education we do not expect everyone to be able to teach nor even to teach children from first grade on. But we do expect people to have a general understanding for how our pedagogy has grown out of our knowledge of human beings and the world. Anthroposophy needs to be met with kind understanding. It would be wrong to assume that everybody should know everything. Rather, the effectiveness of the Anthroposophical Society must lie in creating a general understanding, based on sound common sense, for the strivings of anthroposophy, for what it tries to realize for the welfare and future of humanity.

Blackboard Illustrations

ooooooo *Yellow*
.... *Red*
— — — *White*
—..— *Blue*
—◦— *Green*

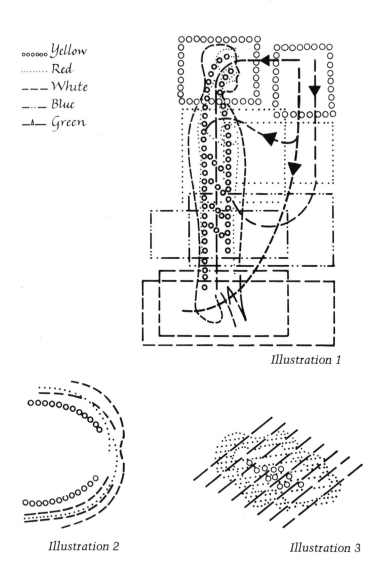

Illustration 1

Illustration 2

Illustration 3

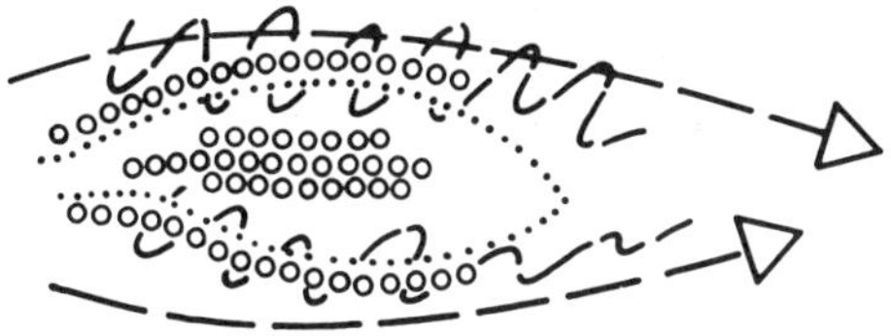

Illustration 4

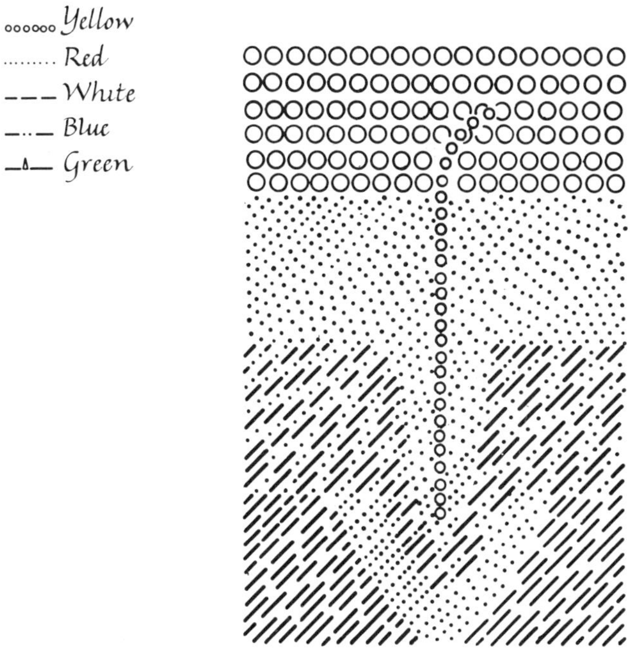

ₒₒₒₒₒₒ *Yellow*
.... *Red*
___ *White*
_..._ *Blue*
_ₐ_ *Green*

Illustration 5

February 16, 1923

MORAL IMPULSES AND THEIR PHYSICAL MANIFESTATIONS: TAKING UP A SPIRITUAL PATH

PART I

TODAY I would like to add some comments to what I said in previous lectures about the task of anthroposophy now and in the future development of humanity. In particular, I want to consider the perspective we get when we look at how Friedrich Nietzsche led the philosophy of the nineteenth century into absurdity.[1] We can show that Nietzsche, more than anyone else, demonstrates that the anthroposophical view of human beings and the world is a historical necessity in human evolution. I do not want to repeat what I have already said about Nietzsche, both here and elsewhere in the anthroposophical movement; rather, I want to talk about two influences on his philosophy that I have not yet talked about.

Throughout his life, Nietzsche was preoccupied with forming an opinion about the nature and value of moral impulses in human beings. He was a moral philosopher in the true sense of the word. He wanted to get a clear idea of the origin and significance of morality, both for the individual and for the whole cosmic order. In his striving for clarity on this issue two elements run like a red thread through his whole life—a life that changed considerably in many other respects.

The first of these factors is that, beginning with the turning point in his second year at the university until the end of his life, Nietzsche basically had an atheistic outlook, which remained unchanged through all the transformations of his philosophy. The second factor is that in regard to the moral, intellectual, and practical impulses of his time, he asserted that *one* virtue was the most important, namely, honesty—honesty with oneself, with others, and with the world as a whole. He considered honesty the most essential virtue modern people needed to have both inwardly in their own soul and outwardly in the world.

Nietzsche once listed four cardinal virtues he considered most important for human life. Honesty with oneself and others was first on his list. The other three were: courage toward one's enemies, magnanimity to those one has defeated, and courtesy to everyone. These four cardinal virtues can ultimately be reduced to the first, which Nietzsche considered a kind of necessary virtue of the times; they are all contained, so to speak, in honesty. We can say that there is a relationship between this virtue of honesty and his atheism.

Nietzsche was first and foremost a child of his time. Even at a superficial glance we see that he was rooted in Schopenhauer's world view, which was also an atheist outlook,[2] and, at least in the first period of his life, he saw Richard Wagner's musical dramas as the artistic expression of Schopenhauer's world view.[3] Then Nietzsche took up the scientific positivism of the times, that is, the philosophy that believes the whole world is built up exclusively from what is directly perceptible to the senses. For positivism, the sense-perceptible world is the only standard for developing a philosophy. In his third period, Nietzsche achieved a certain independence through assimilating the modern idea of evolution, which he elaborated and applied to human beings by developing the positivist ideal of the evolution of the human being into "superman."

Thus, Nietzsche's views grew out of various cultural currents of his time. Investigating how his views developed will also reveal important aspects of the character of the last third of the nineteenth century. We have to ask why Nietzsche became an atheist. His atheism developed out of his honesty, his inner honesty. After all, with holy zeal and complete honesty, Nietzsche took in everything he could of the knowledge the nineteenth century had to offer. He had to admit that honestly accepting the outlook of the nineteenth century would not lead him to the divine. Therefore he felt he had to eliminate God from his thinking.

This marks the first major conflict between Nietzsche and his age; as a result he became a rebel against his times. Nietzsche saw that most people who had adopted the knowledge and outlook of the nineteenth century also believed in a divine world order. To Nietzsche, this was dishonest. It seemed to him dishonest to look at the world from the prevailing point of view of that time and, at the same time, to assume the existence of a deity.

Since he was still expressing himself in the formulas typical for nineteenth century thought, Nietzsche did not actually say what he instinctively felt about the nineteenth century world view. He felt the nineteenth century looked at the world just as it does at the human organism when it has become a corpse. If you believe, so to speak, in this dead organism, if you think it has an inner reality, then, if you are honest, you cannot also believe that this organism has a meaning only when it is filled with the living, ensouled, and spiritual human being. When we examine a corpse, we really should admit that what we see and examine there is not, strictly speaking, a reality. It is a reality only when it is filled by the human spirit. It needs the human spirit. But this spirit is no longer there in the corpse.

Although Nietzsche did not say it in so many words, he thought that looking at nature in the way modern knowledge does is treating it as a corpse. He felt people should realize that nature, as they see it, no longer contains anything divine. If we are going to accept this view of nature as absolute and speak of nature only in terms of its laws, then we obviously must deny that it has a divine foundation. For according to this view, nature has just as little a divine foundation as a corpse has human spirit in it. This is what lived in Nietzsche's soul. Nevertheless, the nineteenth century world view had such a strong influence on him that he came to believe that nature is all we have, that modern times have taught us not to have anything else. If we adhere to this knowledge of nature, we must reject God.

Thus, Nietzsche considered it dishonest to believe in God and, at the same time, accept modern knowledge. In this regard the life of his soul is extremely interesting precisely because he strove to be so absolutely honest. To believe in God and at the same time accept the prevailing view of nature was, in Nietzsche's eyes, the great lie of nineteenth century culture. Still, he took seriously the natural order that was generally accepted. In fact, he realized that modern life had developed to the point where people adopted this view of nature as a matter of course. It is not that nature had compelled people to accept this order of things; rather, life had become such that this was the only view of nature it could bear. The prevailing view of nature had actually developed out of life itself; yet Nietzsche felt this life was utterly dishonest, and he strove for honesty.

He had to admit that if we live in this order and consider it true, then, within the framework of this truth, we can never become aware of our humanity. Nietzsche's fundamental feeling in the first period of his life was doubt about how he could feel himself a human being when he was confined by the prevailing view of the natural order. The truth, as he saw it, kept him from reaching awareness of his own humanity. That was how Nietzsche felt, and therefore he reached the conclusion in this first period of his life that if he could not live in the realm of truth and reality, he would have to live in that of appearances, in poetry, in art.

Nietzsche believed he had found in the ancient Greeks the nation that had arrived at the same dissatisfaction with the truth out of a certain naiveté and had therefore consoled itself with appearances, with beauty. He expressed this in his first work, *The Birth of Tragedy and the Genealogy of Morals*, which is like a hymn and written very beautifully.[4] He wanted to say that when we are in the realm of reality, we can never be aware of our humanity. Therefore, we should flee from that realm into the one where we can create a world that does not conform to reality. In this world of poetry we will find consolation for what reality can never give us.

According to Nietzsche, the ancient Greeks had been genuine, naive pessimists who felt that they could not be satisfied with the world of reality. That is the main reason why they created their wonderful tragedies—a world of beautiful illusions—to find there what would satisfy them. Nietzsche believed that Wagner's musical dramas were a renewal of this world of beautiful illusions and had been created for the express purpose of leading people from the so-called real world into that of appearances so they could find satisfaction as human beings. Nietzsche thought it was impossible to deepen our study and knowledge of the sensory world and move from the outer revelation to the divine within nature in order to feel ourselves connected with the divine and to feel ourselves as human beings, as *real* in the world.

Nietzsche could not take that approach. He was determined to be honest, and in his honesty he saw no way to arrive at such an approach on the basis of what the nineteenth century had to offer. Thus, he had to stay with the other approach: There is no satisfaction for us in all of reality; therefore let us find satisfaction in an unreal world. Nietzsche's earliest attitude toward the world can be compared to that of beings who land on another planet where they find only corpses. Regarding the corpses not as remains of a reality but as a reality in themselves because the souls that once filled these dead bodies are no longer present, these beings then proceed to make up, for their consolation, fictitious entities to ensoul the corpses.

Basically, Nietzsche's writings following his *The Birth of Tragedy*, for example, "David Strauss the Confessor and Writer," "On the Uses and Disadvantages of History for Life," "Schopenhauer as Educator," and "Richard Wagner in Bayreuth," were confrontations between the dishonesty of his time and his own honesty.[5] Though it had no way out of the sensory realm into the spirit, Nietzsche's age still talked about spirit. Though its knowledge did not really include anything divine, that age still talked about God. In fact, in Nietzsche's time the prevailing view was that in earlier ages people had accepted the illusion of a God, but the study of nature had since revealed that God did not exist—but oh, well, there were concerts and music instead.

This philistine point of view was set forth in one chapter of David Friedrich Strauss's book *The Old and the New Faith*.[6] Nietzsche was particularly annoyed about this chapter, so he wrote an article against Strauss, a relatively excellent man, labeling him a philistine. In this article, Nietzsche explained that people either are dishonest in still assuming the existence of God, or they sink to the level of the banal and philistine, as David Friedrich Strauss did.

However, then followed the second period in Nietzsche's life. He remained true to himself in regard to his atheism and his insistence on honesty. Still, in the earlier period he had accepted ideals, albeit aesthetic ones. He had found them a solace against the reality our outer senses present to us. However, in the second period, Nietzsche clung more strongly to the one and only thing that, according to the prevailing opinion of his time, the world could reveal. He had to admit that, regardless of our devotion to ideals, they are undoubtedly born out of our physical nature. People lead themselves to believe in all kinds of beautiful things, but their ideals and beauty are only all too human.

This was the beginning of the time in Nietzsche's life when he became especially aware of human weaknesses, the all too human, our surrender to our physical nature. Since Nietzsche took the prevailing view of nature seriously, he had to realize that people cannot help but surrender to their physical nature. In fact, at one time he said, "Three cheers for the physical, but let us cheer even more the honesty in our faith in the physical."[7]

In this second phase of his life, Nietzsche said roughly, let us be honest and let us realize that even the most beautiful and idealistic thought we might have is still nothing more than an emanation from our physical nature. Therefore, let us approach human life not by describing the smoke coming out at the top but by looking at the fuel causing the smoke. Then we will arrive not at the idealistic-divine, but at the human, all too human.

In a sense, then, Nietzsche killed every idealistic striving in life because he wanted to be honest with himself and others. He concluded that what people usually call soul is really only a lie. It is actually based on the bodily organization, and the effects of this organization manifest in such a way that we call them "soul." According to Nietzsche, the fact that some of his contemporaries were reading writers such as Voltaire was an indication of true enlightenment.[8] True enlightenment for him meant that people would stop getting themselves entangled in some kind of an illusory world to transcend reality and, instead, would look at the physical nature of reality and see that everything moral originates there.

The most striking feature of the third period in Nietzsche's life is the extreme to which he took his honesty—probably out of his by now highly pathological condition. For example, he claimed that if we take our modern knowledge of nature and its laws seriously, then we have to admit that the spirit supposedly living in us is nothing else than a mere emanation from our physical nature. Therefore, the perfect human being is the one whose physical body is the most perfect in comparison to other parts of the person. In other words, the perfect human being, according to Nietzsche, is the one whose physical nature is such that the strongest instincts live in him.

Nietzsche believed the instinctual life rather than the life of soul and spirit would lead us beyond ourselves in our evolution, because the instincts, though remaining just instincts, nevertheless would become stronger and stronger, grow beyond the level of animal instincts, and then the human race would develop into "superman."[9] Why did Nietzsche first admit that human beings needed the illusion of ideals, then unmask these ideals as emanating from the physical, and then postulate that the human race would evolve into "superman" through a higher development of its physical nature, its instinctual life? He was led to this because he thought people steeped in the world view of the nineteenth century could not possibly understand the physical and yet go beyond it and remain honest at the same time. If they wanted to be honest, they had to stay within the realm of the physical.

Nietzsche then cultivated a strict honesty and completely committed himself with his whole being to the physical realm. Indeed, his ideal for the future of human civilization (if we can call it an ideal) was that human beings would throw light on the grand illusion of having a spirit. People usually are not aware of this background of Nietzsche's views—after all, he worked his way out of all this with the greatest possible honesty by denying the existence of spirit so spiritedly and glorifying the spiritual poverty of humanity so brilliantly and ingeniously.

Within the framework of the world view of the nineteenth century, it was impossible to be a moral philosopher (as Nietzsche had become because of his predisposition) if this world view was accepted honestly and seriously. For if we can no longer say that our task on earth is to bring a spiritual, super-earthly element into this earthly world but believe that we have to confine ourselves to this earthly realm, then we will have no justification for setting up moral standards. If we accept the nineteenth century world view in all honesty, then morality becomes a free-for-all.

And Nietzsche really felt deeply that morality had become a free-for-all. He wanted to be a moral philosopher, but where was he to get moral impulses from? That was the big question. If we see the supersensible illuminating human beings, then morality is what this supersensible element demands of our sensory existence; then morality is possible. However, if we see nothing supersensible in human beings, as the nineteenth century world view did not, there is no source from which we might draw moral impulses. To distinguish between good and evil, we need the supersensible. Thus, Nietzsche groped his way through human life to find a source or origin of moral impulses.

For example, he looked at the history of human civilization and found that strong races conquered weaker people, forcing their standards and norms on these weaker ones. Out of their instincts, the conquerors ordered the defeated people to do this or that. Nietzsche, of course, could not believe in any categorical imperative or moral rules. He could only believe in a race of people of instinct who saw themselves as good and others as bad, inferior people whose actions and standards they could dictate.

Then those who, according to the conquerors, were the inferior people in turn ganged up and conquered the former, not with the older, brutal means, but with the more subtle weapons of the soul and spirit, with cunning and ingenuity. Now they in turn called the former conquerors "bad" because they had been conquerors, despots, musclemen, and militaristic people. On the other hand, the new victors called themselves "good"—formerly they had been considered inferior and bad. To hold one's own in weakness and defeat in spite of being poor, restricted, oppressed, and vanquished: that is good. To conquer and defeat others: that is evil. Thus, "good" and "evil" developed out of "good" and "bad." However, "good" and "bad" did not yet smack of moral judgments as they do now, but merely carried a suggestion of conquering, powerful, and aristocratic people in contrast to the army of slaves who were considered inferior and bad people.

Our distinction between "good" and "evil" derives merely from the slave revolts of those who had formerly been bad and inferior and now called the others criminals and evil and were taking revenge for what had been done to them. Thus, the morality later expressed in the categories "good" and "evil" seemed to Nietzsche to be nothing more than the revenge of the oppressed on their former oppressors. He could find no inner justification for morality, he could only place himself outside the framework of good and evil, not inside it. For to find an inner justification for the categories "good" and "evil," he would have had to reach out to the supersensible. However, to him the supersensible was a delusion, nothing but the expression of our weak human nature refusing to admit that our true being is limited to the physical.

We could say that all thinking people of Nietzsche's time would have had to agree with him if they had been as honest as he. Nietzsche had made it his goal to be completely honest. That is why he became a rebel against his time and had such sharp mental weapons. That is also the reason why he was striving for a transvaluation of all values. To him, the values by which he lived had developed out of dishonesty. Through work done over centuries, the modern scientific concepts had been established and been introduced into history. Yet those same centuries had not taken out of human souls what could not be reconciled with these scientific concepts, namely, ideas about morality and God. Values had developed that now needed to be transvalued.

Nietzsche's life was really a terrible tragedy. I don't think it is possible to understand human civilization in the last third of the nineteenth century, or its lingering effects on the twentieth century, without having at least some insight into this tragedy that took its course in a soul living through that time, a soul such as Nietzsche's. It is really true that all the breakdown we are experiencing now can be seen as a consequence of what Nietzsche called the dishonesty of modern civilization. We could say that Nietzsche became a rebel against his time because he felt that the continuation of this dishonesty would lead to a destructive battle involving all peoples belonging to this modern civilization. Indeed, the tragedy of Nietzsche's life developed because he was looking for the basis of morality, but the education and culture of his time made him unable to find it. He could not find a source from which to draw moral impulses. Thus, he groped his way through life and in the process hurt his fingers. Out of the pain he suffered he described his time the way he did.

Nietzsche was searching for something that cannot be found in the sensory realm but only in the supersensible. After all, you can come up with ever so beautiful, grand, and lofty ideals; yet you cannot fuel an engine, turn a wheel, or start an electric motor with them. When we focus only on what can fuel an engine, start an electric motor, or turn a wheel, we will never understand how the moral impulses living in us can possibly affect our organism. You see, no matter how lofty our ideals, they are, after all, only smoke and mist, for there is no way they can intervene in a muscle, improve any of our skills, or the like.

We cannot see moral ideals intervening in the organic realm anywhere in the sensory world. Nietzsche could not help realizing that when we come up with ever so beautiful ideals and keep them in our heads, we are treating our organism just as we would a machine. As far as machines are concerned, we can write the words "moral ideals" on posters; they will still not fuel the machines nor make them move. Nevertheless, we move, and if we are as natural science sees us, are we then moving in accordance with our moral ideals? Compared to reality, our ideals are lies. The effective person is not the one who is devoted to ideals, but the one who fuels his or her engine so that the instincts become more powerful—the "blond beast," as Nietzsche put it.[10]

These were the problems Nietzsche had to face when confronting a human race that could have been moral according to his definition only if the moral impulses had been able to intervene in them. They had not been able to, and therefore there was neither good nor evil, only *Beyond Good and Evil*.[11]

Now, remember that we have always described the modern knowledge of the world as unable to really understand the human being; it cannot arrive at a clear picture or idea of the human being. Through our experiencing life in our souls in accordance with this modern world view, we cannot come close to knowing the human being. Yet, everything in Nietzsche was directed to the human being; everything was aimed at something he could not reach! In addition, he wanted to lead the human being to develop into "superman" in accordance with the modern idea of human evolution. However, he had not really grasped the human being. Of course, he could not possibly have shown how something he did not have was to develop into "superman." According to Nietzsche, the human being as such did not exist in terms of idea, perception, feeling, or will impulse— and "superman" necessarily even less so! It was as though he had said the words "human being" and "superman" only out of an old habit and was now choking on them because they had no content, just as one would suffocate in an airless room.

Nietzsche was faced with the necessity of entering the supersensible world with his moral problems, but he was unable to do so. That was his inner tragedy, and that is also what makes him a representative of the late nineteenth century. As a representative soul of that age, he indicated that human beings have to enter into the supersensible world if they want to remain honest and not declare moral ideals mere lies. Nietzsche became insane because he was faced with the need to enter the supersensible world but could not do so. Of course, there are many people who do not become insane, but I will not go into the reasons why they don't at this point. After all, even in the description of peculiarities of our civilization we must not overstep the boundaries of courtesy.

Still, we can see one thing clearly from Nietzsche's life: Modern people can be honest with themselves and others only if they enter the supersensible world. In other words, we cannot maintain honesty and sincerity in a world view that is not supersensible. By the same token, we will not find the way from the human being to the "superman" if we cannot take the path from the sensory world to the supersensible one. If morality, in a certain sense, belongs to the "superman," then it demands that we look for this "superman" not in the sensory world but in the supersensible one. Otherwise, the term "superman" is merely an empty word we call out that is not met with any sound from the world.

Tomorrow we will consider this topic from another angle. In particular, we will go into more detail about what

Nietzsche met with so that we can rightly understand moral values in human life and bring them into harmony with the knowledge and outlook of our times.

Moral Impulses and Their Physical Manifestations: Taking Up a Spiritual Path

Part II

TAKING THE example of Nietzsche, who declared himself a moral philosopher, I explained yesterday that people steeped entirely in outer modern civilization will fail in their attempts to find moral impulses in the nature of the human being because present-day knowledge does not tell us how moral impulses intervene in our physical life. On the one hand, our civilization accepts the laws of natural science, which have already influenced our education to such an extent that we absorb their interpretations of nature from childhood on. On the other hand, there is a moral world view that stands on its own. We regard moral impulses as commandments or as standards of behavior developed through social conventions. We are unable to conceive of a close connection between ethics and our physical life. As I pointed out yesterday, Nietzsche made honesty his prime virtue, and, out of his honesty and sincerity, he finally reached the conclusion that human beings are only physical beings. He felt our physical life was human, all too human, and was also the basis of our morality. Because Nietzsche wanted to be honest regarding the world view of his time, he failed in his moral philosophy. He was unable to see where morality and the physical world meet and work together.

Of course, it is impossible to see this working together without entering the realm rightly called the supersensible world. We have to realize that it is only in human life that moral impulses—moral ideals, if you like—and the physical processes and functions within us come into contact. Today, the big question for us is whether the moral impulses we have remain abstract or can actually intervene in our physical organization.

As I said yesterday, we can be sure that no moral impulse intervenes in the mechanism of a machine. There is no direct connection between the moral world order and machines. Consequently, when the human organism is presented as a kind of machine, as happens more and more often in the modern scientific outlook, the same then applies to us, and moral impulses are only an illusion. At best, we can hope that some being, made known to us through revelation, will intervene in the moral world order, reward the good, and punish the evil people. But we cannot see a connection between moral impulses and physical processes inherent in the order of the world.

Today I want to talk about the realm where this connection between the physical and the moral actually exists. To help us understand what I am going to say, we will begin with animals. Their physical body, their organism of etheric formative forces, and their astral body work together. There is no real I incarnated in animals; rather, they have a group-I that intervenes from the outside. Now we must realize that we have to distinguish two main parts in the animal organization. On the one hand, there is the head. In higher animals, and also in human beings, the head is the primary bearer of the nerve-sense organism. Everything the animals take in from the outer world enters their body mainly through the organs in the head. Of course, what I have emphasized so often is true here too: we should not project the organization of an organism as a whole onto one of its physical parts. In a sense, however, animals are all head even though they can perceive with their whole body, not just the head. Their nerve-sense organism is mostly located in their head. That is where their relationship to the outer world develops.

When we now look at the overall organization of animals and see that the opposite pole to the head organism is the tail end, then in terms of the animals' physical, etheric, and astral organization, we can say that their astral mobility flows from the back to the front. The streams of their astral body are continuously flowing from the back to the front and meet the sensory impressions received through the sense organs in the head. Thus, the two streams merge. I can draw you a rough sketch of this; here the astral streams, flowing from the back to the front (red arrows), are met by the sensory impressions flowing from the head toward the tail end (yellow arrows). These two currents merge and work together throughout the animals' organism.

You can see this merging clearly in dogs. Upon seeing its master, a dog wags its tail. This shows the dog received the sensory impression of its master, which flows from the front to the back, and this is now met by the astral stream. This streaming of the whole organism from the back to the front manifests in the wagging of the tail. There is complete harmony. If you want to know how joy is expressed in the

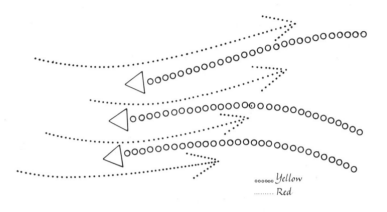

ooooooo _Yellow_

.... _Red_

physiognomy of a dog, you should not look so much at its face when it sees its master but rather at the wagging tail.

Basically, this applies to all animals. In lower species, for example, in fish, we cannot see this as clearly because their astral body is more independent. However, with clairvoyant consciousness we can see it all the more clearly. Clairvoyant consciousness knows that when a fish perceives through its nerve-sense apparatus that something is floating toward it, the fish sends its own astral stream from the back toward the front to meet the impression from the outside. As a result, there is a wonderful glittering merging of what the fish sees and what it brings to meet the perception. This deep meshing of the astral stream from the outside—after all, what a being receives with sensory impressions is an astral stream from the outside—and the astral stream flowing from the back to the front is interrupted in human beings because we stand upright.

Because we are upright beings, we cannot send astral streams to meet our sensory impressions as directly as, for example, dogs can. Dogs have a horizontal spine. Thus, the astral stream from the back to the front goes through their head. Our head stands out, so to speak. Therefore, the relationship between the astral currents flowing from the back to the front (which are what our inner being consists of) and the other ones coming through our sensory impressions is not as simple as it is in animals.

We have to study carefully what I have just explained if we want to understand how the moral intervenes in our physical nature. We do not concede morality to animals because in them the streaming of the astral from back to front and from front to back is not interrupted at all. In human beings, however, the following occurs: Our head is lifted out of the astral current that flows from back to front. This signifies the incarnation of our I. It is because our blood flows not only horizontally but also upward as the bearer of our inner I-forces that we experience this I as our own, individual I. That is also why our head, the main carrier of our sensory impressions, is at first completely focused on the outer world. Due to the way we are organized, our sense of touch is much more loosely connected to that of sight than is the case in animals. When animals see something, they immediately have the feeling of touching what they are looking at. The sense of touch is stimulated by their sight. This stimulation of the sense of touch then combines with the current flowing from the back to the front. In contrast, our head is lifted above this and focused exclusively on the outer world, as is obvious above all in our sense of sight.

In a way, our sense of sight is a kind of etheric sense. For example, we learn only gradually to judge distances and so on, and we mostly see what is expressed in color and shades of color. Just remember that painting in perspective was not developed until the age of intellectualism. Earlier artists did not yet paint in perspective. It was only later, by way of judgment and intellectualism, that human eyes became used to seeing the reality that is expressed in perspective, in distances.

Our eyes see mostly color, contrasts, and shades of light and dark. Light covers all objects; it actually originates in the cosmos. The sun sends out its light, and since the light coming from the cosmos falls on objects on the earth and is reflected by them, our eyes actually do not see things by means of earthly forces but only with the help of cosmic forces.

This is symptomatic of our head in general. It is more open to the etheric element in the world than to the physical. We actually find our way in the physical world more by moving around in it and touching it than by using the sense organs in our head. Imagine how ghostly, how etheric-ghostly, the world would be if we did not find our bearings in space through our sense of touch but had to rely only on what our eyes tell us. Animal heads are organized entirely differently from the human head. The animals' organization is much more closely connected with physical reality through the head than our organization. The perceptions of our head are like ideals because they are etheric. In fact, with our head we live completely in an etheric world.

The outer shape of our head is an image of the cosmos—and this is not a mere superficiality. In contrast, the various shapes of animal heads are a direct expression of the animals' corporeality. You will not find the cosmic rounded shape of the human head in the animal kingdom. Our head is indeed an image of the cosmic spheres. We have developed this shape because we have a vertical body axis and not a horizontal one as the animals do. In a sense, we have risen beyond the horizontal into the vertical.

We can see this especially clearly when we look at our

organization as a whole. The physical organization of our head is attached to an etheric organization that mirrors the purity of the cosmos. The organization of our head in the etheric body is hardly at all in contact with earthly elements throughout our life on earth. In its etheric and even more so in its astral elements it remains completely cosmic. In fact, when we pass on from one earthly life to the next, the rest of our bodily organization, that is, the part below the head, is transformed. It undergoes a metamorphosis, not in its physical matter but in its force constellation, and becomes the head of our next incarnation. Of course, as a system of forces, the head of our present incarnation vanishes after our death. In other words, to develop into head organization, our physical organization first has to go through the cosmos. Our head organization cannot develop on earth. Through our head we are completely open to the cosmos, but through the rest of our organization we are bound to the earthly realm.

The shape of animal heads develops out of the rest of their organization. However, our head in a sense lifts itself with a certain amount of independence out of our organization. Now, the rest of our organization pushes its way into our head in our changing gestures and facial expressions. For example, if you are inwardly agitated because you are frightened, then what is in your metabolism and blood circulation is expressed through the forces of your organism in your changing expressions and the sudden paling of your face. Other emotions affect us similarly. In other words, what lives in the rest of our organism pours soul-spiritually, that is, astrally, into our head. What lives astrally in the rest of our organism becomes manifest in our complexion and, above all, in our changing expressions, in our physiognomy, in the physiognomy and mobility of our head.

It is highly interesting to observe the facial expressions accompanying what somebody is saying to us—which comes from his or her I. We can read in the person's face what lives in his or her astral body. If you observe the face of someone speaking to you, you receive that person's I with his or her words and the other's astral body with the facial expressions accompanying the words. The astral organism of the head, which causes the changing features, is connected to an etheric organism, which is a wonderful image of the cosmos. It is very strange to observe with supersensible sight a person speaking. One sees the astral body making itself felt everywhere in the person's changing features, but the etheric organism of the head is hardly touched at all by the facial expressions. The etheric organism of the head refuses to assimilate the facial expressions into itself, into its forms.

For instance, it is very interesting to see that certain hymns permeate a person's astral body with a feeling of holiness and are easily assimilated into the etheric organization of the head. In the process, the etheric body accompanies the facial expressions with a play of light in its facial region. However, in the parts of the etheric body that lie further back, away from the face, there the etheric body puts up a strong resistance against assimilating any processes from the changing features.

This shows you that while our head is in a way related to the rest of our organism, this connection is governed by certain laws because the etheric body is an image of the cosmos. It wants to maintain this shape of the cosmos and does not want to deviate from it, especially not because of what comes from the passions and instincts of human nature.

Our facial expressions are contingent on our temperament, character, and various soul and physical characteristics. They are visible, but there is still another physiognomy that is even much more vivid, but it is in our unconscious. It is supersensible and beyond the scope of our sensory perception. When you look at our astral body, in particular the part that is connected to the metabolic-limb system that surrounds and permeates our legs and abdomen, you will see a very expressive physiognomy if you have supersensible perception. The strange thing is that this physiognomy is revealed from the outside in. Thus, while the physiognomy accompanying our words and expressing our interest in our surroundings is revealed on the outside, another physiognomy that we are not conscious of is revealed on the inside.

I would like to explain this with a diagram (see drawing below). Here we have a human being; there is the astral body (red) that causes the facial expressions visible on the outside, and here is another part of that same astral body (yellow). In the astral body up here (see drawing, top part), our physiognomy is visible on the outside, but down here in the other part (see drawing, bottom part), we have a physiognomy manifesting entirely on the inside. The latter part of the astral body faces toward the inside. We are usually not aware of this, but it is nevertheless true. Children continuously turn this physiognomy of the lower part of the astral body toward their inside; by the time they become adults, the expressions or features become more or less permanently turned to the inside.

Now let me tell you what is behind all this. When we have an impulse to do what is rightly called a good or moral deed, our inner physiognomy is different from what it would be if we had an impulse to do something evil. We have, in a sense, an ugly physiognomy on the inside when we carry out a selfish deed. After all, all moral deeds are basically

113

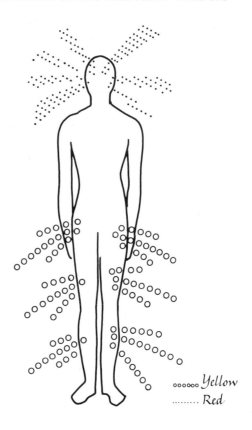

ₒₒₒₒₒₒ *Yellow*
.... *Red*

unselfish, and all immoral ones egotistic. However, in everyday life this moral difference is masked by the fact that people can be very immoral, that is, full of selfish motives, but still follow a conventional code of morality. Of course, this code is not at all their own. Rather, people are stuck in what they were taught since childhood, or in doing things because they are worried about what others will say. True morality, however, that lives in the human individuality means that our good deeds originate in our interest in other people. We can develop this interest by feeling within ourselves what others feel and experience. Basically, immorality means that we close ourselves off against the feelings of others and are unsympathetic. To have morally good thoughts is to put oneself in someone else's place; to have morally evil thoughts is to be unable to do so. This can then develop into laws and conventional rules, things people get embarrassed about—or don't. Actions that are, in fact, selfish can be deeply buried beneath conventions. Fundamentally, however, morality cannot be judged on the basis of what people do; we have to go deeper into the character and nature of human beings to determine the moral value of a person.

Our moral value is expressed in the astral body; its lower part turns a beautiful countenance toward the inside when unselfish deeds and impulses live in us. When selfish and evil impulses live in us, then this part of the astral body turns an ugly countenance toward the inside. Thus, when we can read with spiritual accuracy what is inside a person, we can tell by this physiognomy whether he or she is good or evil, just as we can assess people's other characteristics by their facial expressions. All this is not accessible to our usual consciousness, but it is there nevertheless. It is impossible for dishonesty not to enter deeply into the dishonest person. Now, an out-and-out villain may have complete control over his facial expressions and have the most innocent face you can imagine while he is plotting more villainy; yet, what is in his astral body, in his inner physiognomy and features, he cannot disguise. There he turns into a regular devil the moment his immoral motives appear. On the outside such a villain may seem as innocent as a baby, but inside he looks like a devil; as a pure egotist, he grins diabolically at his own heart. This law applies as much as the natural laws.

Now, the crucial point is that when an ugly physiognomy develops down here (see lower part of drawing), the head, being used to the cosmos, repels it and does not take it in. As a result, we form in our etheric a body, similar to Ahriman's, its atrophied head reduced to the instinctual. Everything goes into the lower members of the etheric body. The head will not accept any of it, and we then become ahrimanic in the lower part of our etheric body. Then our head, too, becomes permeated with what this ahrimanic body pushes up into it. The strange thing here is that our head, already in its warmth ether, rejects the physiognomy of immorality and does not let it enter.

Consequently, immoral people have an etheric-ahrimanic organism within them, but the shape and function of their head is not influenced by that. Their head is still an image of the cosmos, but it is less and less a part of them because they cannot permeate it with their own being. Immoral people do not advance far beyond their previous incarnation. Their head, developed through the transformation of the rest of their body from the preceding incarnation, remains unchanged; thus, they have not advanced much by the time they die.

On the other hand, the inner effects of our moral imagination create a vertical stream up into our head. Nothing immoral can stream in the vertical direction. It is pushed back, pressed together, and makes the person ahrimanic. Only what is moral can stream in the vertical direction. In fact, the physiognomy of the immoral is repelled in its vertical movement already in the etheric, already in the warmth ether of the blood. Our head does not take it in. However, the moral enters our head with the warmth of the blood already in the warmth ether, and even more so in the light ether, the chemical ether, and the life ether. Then we permeate our head with our own being.

What happens there is indeed an intervention of the moral in the physical organization, for we can say that our etheric head organization has an affinity for the moral in us but not for the immoral. Of course, if we do not go beyond physical, sensory perception, we cannot see how our moral impulses work into our physical organization by way of the etheric. We have to look at the human being as a whole, including the etheric and astral organization, to see how the moral intervenes in the human organism.

As you can imagine, this looks different when we are dead. If our head has repelled the forces of our remaining organization, then in our etheric body, which we cast off after a few days, there will be nothing left of us. Then we cannot have much of an effect on the world, and we cannot work on the further development of the earth because we do not send forces into what will last into the future. If we have developed moral impulses that have entered our head, then our etheric body leaves us after death in the form of a human being.

The etheric body of immoral persons, on the other hand, looks completely ahrimanic when it leaves them. We can get a good idea of the shape of Ahriman even without trying to meet Ahriman himself; we only need to look at the etheric body of immoral persons, whose form has become completely ahrimanic, merging into the cosmos. However, the etheric body that leaves the I and the astral body of a moral individual two or three days after death will be humanized, well-rounded, and serene.

Such individuals assimilate their experiences during life with their head, and through the head's resemblance to the cosmos, they can then give them to the cosmos. As I said, our head resembles the cosmos, but the rest of our organism does not. Instead, after it has been given over to the cosmos, the rest of our organism will be scattered and fall back onto the earth or enter streams that circle the earth. However, our morality that we have imprinted into our head will be poured out into the cosmos, and that is how we participate in the reshaping of the cosmos.

In other words, by being moral or immoral we actively work on the future of the earth. Immoral people present the forces surrounding the earth with what drizzles down onto the earth etherically and reunites with it, or what lives in the orbit around the earth. These surrounding forces are important for all earth activity because the physical of the earth develops eventually out of the etheric. On the other hand, moral people have taken into their head the forces that develop especially through moral impulses, and they therefore give to the cosmos what they have achieved on earth.

If we remain within the limits of the earth, we cannot see how moral impulses actually work; they remain only abstractions for us. For example, consider what a moral philosopher such as Herbart says about moral impulses.[1] He distinguishes five kinds of moral impulses: inner freedom, benevolence, perfection, fairness, and honesty. People living according to these five virtues would be moral people for Herbart. However, Herbart is unable to say anything more concrete and specific. He can only characterize an individual as moral; he cannot explain what this means for the world.

Yesterday I told you about the four cardinal virtues Nietzsche distinguished; his grouping is a bit different from Herbart's. Nietzsche listed honesty with oneself and one's friends, courage toward one's enemies, magnanimity toward the vanquished, and courtesy to everyone. Other moral philosophers have listed other virtues. However, all these virtues remain abstractions as long as we look at the human being only as a physical organism. In a sense, presenting people with these virtues as moral impulses is like giving an order to a machine. You can persuade and coax a machine all you want—it will not dream of accepting any of your impulses. Similarly, human beings, as they are defined by our modern world view, cannot accept any moral impulses. To understand the reality and effectiveness of the moral we have to enter the supersensible realm. The physiognomy turned toward the inside, the gesture turned inward—they are supersensible. Depending on whether they are moral or immoral, they are either taken in or rejected by the head, and then either flow into the cosmos or shatter on the earth, burst, and are scattered everywhere.

Thus, even a moral philosopher with the inner force of Nietzsche is at loose ends with his moral principles; he can only solidify them in the way I described yesterday. However, that would still not be a true solidity. In spite of all his explanations in *Beyond Good and Evil*, he had to trace everything to the physical body.[2] That is why he failed. Thus, to understand the effectiveness of the moral we have to go beyond the merely physical order of the world and enter the supersensible realm. We have to realize that while morality radiates into the physical in an abstract way, we can understand and assess its activity only in the realm of the supersensible.

February 18, 1923

MORAL IMPULSES AND THEIR PHYSICAL MANIFESTATIONS: TAKING UP A SPIRITUAL PATH PART III

AS I have often emphasized, intellectual life has become predominant in our time. Preparations for this began during the fourth post-Atlantean or Greco-Roman epoch. As you know, on the basis of certain human soul characteristics that developed during that time, we have to say that the Greco-Roman period lasted from the eighth century B.C. to the fifteenth century A.D. It was followed by the period of soul development for western humanity we live in now.

The relationship of people to the intellectual world was different prior to the fifteenth century. Although the inclination in the mood of human souls toward intellectualism that existed in Greece has been in decline since the fourth century A.D., the Greco-Roman soul mood can still be detected everywhere in the second part of the fourth post-Atlantean epoch. To fully understand this particular soul mood, we have to put ourselves with all our heart and mind into the ancient Greeks. This applies particularly to the special characteristics they had during the age lasting from Socrates and Plato to the decline of Hellenism.

What shines through ordinary and superficial history tells us—even if we are not steeped in spiritual science—that when the ancient Greeks attained an intellectual view of the world, they felt joy, or at least satisfaction, about having advanced in their humanity. They believed that having gone through the various stages of education at that time and being able to form a world view through the power of their intellect meant they had progressed to a higher stage of humanity. They felt that they were human beings in a higher sense when they could grasp the world intellectually. Thus, there existed a complete joy and satisfaction in intellectual life.

We find this also in later epochs, for instance, in John Scotus Erigena, who lived in the ninth century A.D.[1] The way he formulated and presented his ideas shows that he believed people would feel enthusiasm about understanding them. This was still very much the case with those people who tried to attain an intellectual world view in the isolation from the world typical of scholasticism—even though by then their discussions had become less heated. It is only in these last few centuries that people have begun believing they will lose their soul warmth when they become intellectual. As recently as the time of Schiller and his intellectual world view, or of Goethe and his extraordinarily exact morphology, things were quite different.[2] People such as these two great personalities developed an idealistic intellectual world view and believed they were not truly human until they could bring inner warmth into their ideas.

It is only quite recently that people have begun to perceive the world of ideas as cold and pale. In accordance with an important law in human evolution, people's relationship to the world of intellectually formed ideas has changed drastically. In earlier times, the world of ideas was concerned with life and the living. People believed the cosmos was alive. True insight into ancient concepts and thoughts reveals that people back then saw everything that was dead as a kind of precipitate of the living substance they believed to be spread out over the whole world. In other words, what was dead was regarded like the ashes that are left over when something is burned. In those days, people had a very different feeling about the universe than we do. To them, the universe was a big, living organism, and everything that was dead, for example, the mineral realm, was like the ashes that precipitated out from the world processes. It was dead because it was a waste product or residue of everything living.

This feeling about the world has changed tremendously over the last few centuries. Scientific knowledge is highly respected, or at least it has usually been highly respected, as long as the scientists expounded only on what is dead. And increasingly, people have felt the longing to see life itself as only a chemical combination of dead elements. Thus, the idea of the spontaneous generation of life out of dead matter developed.

As I have often explained, the medieval representation of homunculus in a retort as a being made up of various ingredients was not meant as a picture of spontaneous generation in the sense recent natural scientists use that term. Rather, this representation was intended to depict the conjuring forth of a particular living creature out of the indefinite living universe. People then did not yet conceive of the universe as a mechanism, as something dead, and that is why they believed it was possible to bring forth a particular living being out of the indefinite life of the world. People in the Middle Ages did not yet think of combining dead elements to create life. Without spiritual science, these things are hard to understand nowadays because people have gotten used to thinking their concepts have become perfect and absolutely right after having passed through various childhood stages of humanity.

We can talk about modern progress all we want; it is still true that people have never been as rigid in their concepts and thoughts as they are now. It is ultimately a subjective element that makes people so rigid, particularly in their understanding and knowledge. What is dead remains entirely passive when we apply our ideas and concepts to it. Thus, we can develop our concepts quite nicely and comfortably, for the dead element is not going to object or resist. We can then apply our concepts about the physical world to nature without being bothered by the fact that nature itself in its living flexibility challenges us to be just as flexible in our concepts. Goethe still felt that our concepts had to be inwardly alive, without sharply defined contours. Only then can our concepts adapt and adjust to the living, flexible world and to living and flexible beings.

To put it in a somewhat paradoxical way, people nowadays prefer their concepts to be convenient. However, rigid concepts with sharply defined contours can be applied only to what is dead and does not budge, thus allowing our concepts to remain rigid. Nevertheless, living in rigid concepts that ignore everything living has given us the opportunity to attain an inner awareness of freedom, as I have often explained.

Two developments have come about as a result of our concepts having become dead: first, the awareness of freedom, and second, the possibility to apply the rigid concepts, which have been developed out of what is dead and can be used only for what is dead, in our magnificent, triumphant technology, which is nothing more than the putting into practice of a rigid system of ideas. This is one aspect of the evolution modern humanity has undergone. We have to understand how human beings, in a sense, have cut themselves off from everything living, that the living has become alien to them. And we also have to understand that when we do not want to remain in the realm of the dead, but want to take the impulse of the living into our soul, then we must find this living element on our own.

In very ancient times, people saw life in every cloud formation, every flash of lightning, every roll of thunder, in every living plant, and so on. In a sense, they breathed in life and thus understood it, and without any effort they were in the midst of life. They only had to take in life from the outside. In contrast, in our evolutionary stage our concepts can grasp only what is dead, and the outer environment can no longer give us what is alive. Therefore, we must bring forth this living element out of the innermost core of our being.

It is not enough to understand history merely theoretically, with our intellect, for then history appears much too uniform and unvarying. We have to put ourselves with all our soul into the way people in past epochs experienced history. Then we will see that a tremendous change took place between the pre-Grecian ages, which we trace back to Atlantean times in our anthroposophy—that is, to the seventh and eighth millennia B.C.—the Greek age, and our own time. Today I would like to talk concretely and in detail about this change in people's attitudes toward the universe. I want to describe this change from the vantage point of spiritual vision.

In early history, for example, in the Egyptian or the Babylonian-Chaldean culture, or even in the ancient Persian culture, people believed they had descended to earth from a pre-earthly life. They felt they were bearing within them the aftereffects of what the gods had implanted in them during this pre-earthly life. Of course, ordinary history tells us only very little about these times; we need to use the methods of spiritual science to penetrate and understand these things.

In those times people expressed their relationship to the earth by saying: Here I stand on earth. Before this, I was in a soul-spiritual world, a world of light, so to speak. That light continues to shine mysteriously within me. In a sense, as a human being, I am a vessel for the divine light that continues to live within me.

In other words, people were aware that a divine element had come down to earth with them. They did not say (and this can be proved philologically) I stand upon the earth, but they said: As a human being, I am a vessel for the God who has come to the earth. That is what was in people's consciousness in early history.

In fact, the further back we go in evolution, the more prevalent is the awareness that the human being is a vessel for the God who has descended to earth. The divine element then was manifold. To the ancient consciousness, the lowest gods in the divine hierarchy that extended all the way down to the earth were the human beings themselves. If we do not present a distorted picture of oriental culture, as Deussen has done in such a terribly superficial way, but really try to sympathize with the consciousness of the ancient Indians when they felt their Brahma within them, felt themselves enveloping it, then we will understand what human soul life in ancient times was really like.[3]

Out of this consciousness developed the feelings people

had for the Divine Father, the Father God. People felt themselves to be, in a sense, the sons and daughters of the gods. They did not feel this way about their physical body, but only about what this physical body enveloped. Some people in ancient times thought that our flesh and blood indeed was not worthy to be a vessel for a god. Thus, it was not the human being of flesh and blood that they regarded as divine, but the part that projected from the spiritual world into this physical-earthly human being, into the human being of flesh and blood.

People felt their relationship to the Father God was a religious one. The highest rank in the ancient Mysteries was that of father. In most oriental Mysteries, the candidates had to advance through seven stages. The first stage was one of preparation. Here the candidates had to develop the soul mood that would enable them to understand what was shown to them in the Mysteries. In the second through the fourth stages, the candidates achieved a full understanding of their folk soul. As a result they no longer felt themselves to be isolated individuals but members of a group or community. As they advanced to the fifth and sixth stages, the candidates felt themselves more and more to be vessels of the divine element.

The highest stage was that of the father. The candidates who reached this stage were personalities who represented in their outer life what people felt to be the divine primordial principle to which they really felt connected. Their culture was completely determined by the center of their religious life: people had to consciously feel a relationship to the divine fatherly creative principle. Accordingly, people felt everything they could understand within themselves, for example, the light of knowledge they could become aware of, as bequeathed upon them by God the Father. They felt God the Father continuing to work in their intellect. All their cults were shaped by this as they were simply reflections of the path of knowledge the candidates took in the Mysteries.

Then came the age of Greek antiquity. The ancient Greeks were the purest representative of the stage of humanity that developed out of the soul conditions I have just described. The Greeks thought of themselves more as human beings than as mere vessels of the divine. Nevertheless, their feeling about themselves was such that those who had undergone any education—let's say intellectual, artistic, or religious training—felt that the divine had completely entered into the human being, without remainder, so to speak. Thus, they no longer thought of themselves as vessels of a god, but rather as representations of him.

However, this was not expressed as openly as the other soul condition had been in earlier times. In ancient Greece, it was revealed only to Mystery candidates at a certain stage of initiation that as human beings they were also divine beings, sons of the gods. In fact, it was considered impossible to present this mystery of the origins of humanity to people who were unprepared. Nevertheless, this was how the initiated Greeks thought, and thus it was the fundamental feeling of their culture. It was not a sharply defined idea, but a basic feeling of the soul. This basic feeling is expressed in Greek art, where the gods are represented as idealized human beings in accordance with that fundamental feeling. In a sense, then, the ancient Greeks kept their relationship to the divine in the purity of their heart and feelings.

Now, when the Greek world view was well into its decline, a totally new soul mood appeared with the fifteenth century. People no longer thought of themselves as earthly vessels of the divine or as representations of the divine.

127

Instead, they saw themselves as having evolved through lower, imperfect stages into human beings—beings who can only look up to the otherworldly divine. The natural sciences of modern times are based on this fundamental feeling, but we have not yet been able to understand how these sciences are related to ourselves. It is the task of anthroposophy to help us find once again this relationship to ourselves and to the divine. This refinding can be accomplished in the following way.

Imagine what people in pre-Grecian ages felt in their soul. They would have felt that they enveloped a divine element. By enveloping the divine with their flesh and blood, they could not help but represent it on earth in less than its true dignity and glory. In a sense, they could not help degrading it. In order to represent the divine element within them in all its purity, they had to purify themselves; they had to undergo a kind of catharsis or purification so that the divine within them would be the predominating element.

Basically, this is nothing else than a return to the fatherly primordial principle, as we see it in many religions of antiquity where people believed that after death they would return to their ancestors, even their remote ancestors. In all religions there is this longing to return to the divine father's primordial creative principle. It indicates that human beings did not yet feel at home on earth. At the same time, they did not yet see themselves as completely separate from God and moving longingly toward the otherworldly divine out of this position of separateness. Rather, people in those early times strove to represent the human being in all his purity because they believed God would then come to light.

All this changed in Greek antiquity. People then no longer felt as closely connected with the divine Father principle as they had in earlier times. They still felt connected to the divine, but at the same time also to the earthly realm. In a sense, people back then felt themselves to be equally close to the divine and to the earthly. This was the age in which the Mystery of Golgotha took place. It was the epoch when in addition to saying "In the beginning was the Word, and the Word was with God," referring to the Father God, "and the Word was God,"(John 1:1)—people had to say "And the Word became flesh." (John 1:14) The Word or Logos had originally been regarded only as the union with the Father God, but now people believed that the Word had fully taken up His abode within human beings; people had to seek Him within themselves. The Mystery of Golgotha fit in very well with this mood of soul. People had never been able to think of God the Father in human form. He had to be thought of purely spiritually. Christ, the Son of God, was conceived of as divine and human at the same time. Basically, what the ancient Greeks longed for or realized in their art was fulfilled for all of humanity in the Mystery of Golgotha in its entirety. We must not be distracted by trivialities but must concentrate on the essentials, namely, the fact that a divine being has entered human beings here on earth.

This makes the Mystery of Golgotha the center of human evolution on earth. It is certainly no mere coincidence that the Mystery of Golgotha took place at the time when the ancient Greeks tried to represent the divine element in human beings from the outside, from the point of view of the earth. It is not just a poetic metaphor to say that in ancient Greek art God was represented as a human being with the ingredients available on earth. And the cosmos sent God down into the human being in order to answer the wonderful question ancient Greek civilization had sent out into the universe, as it were. From human historical development we get the feeling that with their human representations of

the gods the ancient Greeks were asking the cosmos
whether God could become human. And the cosmos an-
swered that God could become human by letting the Mystery of Golgotha take place.

I have often emphasized that we cannot understand this
Mystery of Golgotha in its true essence when we approach
it only with the knowledge about dead things that has become so widespread recently. Rather, we must approach it
with a new, living way of knowing, a way of knowing that
is permeated by spirit. Then we will have to realize that we
have achieved our consciousness of freedom as well as our
technological progress with the help of our dead concepts;
however, we cannot stop with this inner condition of death.
Out of our own soul we must develop the impulse of something living, something alive and spiritual; in other words,
we must be able to have ideas that are inwardly alive. These
ideas must take hold not only of our intellect but of our
whole being.

As I indicated in my book *Goethe's Conception of the
World*, we have to be able once again to advance beyond
dead and abstract concepts to a spirituality that will fill us
with ideas.[4] Into this world of ideas we must then bring all
living warmth that can glow in our soul and all bright light
that can arouse the enthusiasm of our soul. We must become able once again to take up into the realm of ideas all
our soul warmth and all our soul light. We must become
able to inwardly take our whole being with us into the spirituality of the world of ideas. This ability is what we have
lost in our time.

There is probably hardly anything in modern literature
as deeply moving as the first chapter in Nietzsche's presentation of Greek philosophy in "the tragic age of the Greeks"
as he called it.[5] Nietzsche describes the philosophers of the

pre-Socratean age, among them Thales, Heraclitus, and Anaxagoras.[6] If you have a sense for this and have an open mind, you will be very moved by Nietzsche's description of how at a certain point in their development the ancient Greeks rose to the abstraction of pure being. They moved from the manifoldness of the impressions of nature that had filled them with warmth to the pale thought of being. Roughly, Nietzsche said the following: You feel chilly, you feel you enter icy regions, as you follow an ancient Greek philosopher, for example, Parmenides, to this abstract idea of all-embracing being.[7] Nietzsche felt transported from the modern culture—in which he was thoroughly steeped, as I explained here the day before yesterday—into the glacier region of the soul.

In fact, Nietzsche failed because he could only go as far as the coldness, the glacial nature, of the world of ideas. Clairvoyance in true spirituality, however, can bring both soul warmth and soul light into intellectuality; as a result we can achieve the purity in our concepts I have described in *The Philosophy of Freedom*.[8] This purity in our concepts makes us not into inwardly dried-up but rather inwardly enthusiastic human beings. We become able to feel the sun warmth of the cosmos through the cold regions of intellectualism as we leave behind the earthly warmth of the sensory world. We become able to receive the cosmic light through carrying our living soul impulses into the darkness that grows within us as we leave behind the shining earthly objects and enter the world of intellectual concepts—in other words, we become human beings who have overcome the earthly darkness.

Everywhere in Nietzsche's work we can see his longing for this cosmic light and this cosmic warmth. But he could not reach them, and that is why he failed. Anthroposophy wants to show us the way that does not lead to a loss of earth warmth and earth light, but to the preservation of our lively interest in every concrete earthly detail. In other words, we can retain our loving attachment to all earthly things and yet rise to the level of concepts where the divine reveals itself in pure concepts. We modern people can no longer feel the divine element within us, as ancient people still could; we must work to reach the divine realm.

This mood enables us to get the right feeling for the Mystery of the Holy Spirit. Indeed, this is the difference between the spiritual life of modern and ancient people. In ancient times, people drew their spirituality from the many beings of nature. Clouds spoke to them of the spirit, and so did the flowers. In contrast, our concepts have grown cold and dead, and we must bring them to life by ourselves. Only then can we approach the Holy Spirit who will help us to understand the Mystery of Golgotha in the right way.

We take something of our humanity with us when we imbue our ideas with soul warmth and soul light through anthroposophy. If we did not do this, we could not go beyond the dry, banal, and abstract aspect of the world of ideas. When we achieve an understanding of the world through the insights I have explained in my anthroposophical books, then our ideas remain just as exact as they are in mathematics or in the other sciences. Our thinking will be no less exact than that of the chemist in his laboratory or the biologist in his study, but our concepts require that we bring something of ourselves to them. When anthroposophists speak out of Imagination or Inspiration and people really understand them based on their sound common sense, then they will see this Imagination or Inspiration as clearly before them as mathematicians see their equations or geometrical figures. But people must bring something of their humanity with them or they will not understand these ideas in the right way. What they must bring with them is love.

We cannot acquire the knowledge anthroposophy gives us without permeating it with love. Without love it has no more significance than anything else. It makes no difference whether you classify beings as the materialistic scientists do into marsupials, anthropoid apes, ape-men, and human beings or whether you say human beings consist of physical body, etheric body, astral body, and I. Granted, they are different thoughts, but the state of the soul is the same in both cases. The condition of our soul will change only when our spiritual understanding of our place in nature becomes inwardly alive.

It can change only when the same feeling, perception, and soul conditions that live in love also accompany the act of knowing. When we permeate our knowledge with the experience of love, then our knowledge can approach the Mystery of Golgotha. Then we will have more than the naive leaning toward Christ, which in principle is perfectly justified. We will also have a knowledge that extends over the whole cosmos and that can be deepened into an understanding of the Mystery of Golgotha. In other words, life in the Holy Spirit leads to living in Christ, the Son of God.

There we will come to realize that through the Mystery of Golgotha the Logos has passed from the Father to the Son. Then the important insight will be revealed to us that it was right for people in ancient times to say, "In the beginning was the Logos, and the Logos was with God, and the Logos was God." But in Greek antiquity, people had to begin saying, "And the Logos was made flesh." And we modern people must add, "I must achieve an understanding of the Logos living in the flesh by raising my concepts and ideas, my whole world view, into the spiritual realm. Then I will find Christ through the Holy Spirit, and through Christ I will find the Father God." This is definitely not just a theory, but something we can experience directly. This attitude toward Christianity is a natural outgrowth of anthroposophy.

Indeed, it is essential for us in our time to understand such a spiritual path. We need this understanding precisely to counterbalance the dead culture that consists of modern life's mechanism, which we must not disparage but highly appreciate. However, for us modern people to enter upon this spiritual path requires an inner jolt—I have recently called it a true awakening—and many people do not want to make that effort. It is this unwillingness to make the effort of the jolt in one's soul that causes the present-day opposition to anthroposophy. After all, experiencing this jolt is somewhat uncomfortable. In a sense, this jolt pulls us into the maelstrom of cosmic becoming. Of course, people prefer to remain peacefully with their rigid, sharply defined concepts that apply only to what is dead, to what does not put up any resistance to their understanding of the world. In contrast, what is living resists being comprehended with dead concepts; it moves around and eludes our concepts. Modern people find that feeling uncomfortable. They clothe it in all kinds of other things, and they get furious when they hear that certain circles want a very different understanding of the world in all areas of life. It is only on the basis of this attitude that we can understand the peculiar developments among the opponents of anthroposophy. We need only mention a few of the most recent developments and you will clearly see how peculiar they are.

First, there is the tragedy of the loss of our Goetheanum. We know very well that no matter what we can do in the way of rebuilding, the old Goetheanum will not appear again; it will remain only a memory. It is really very painful to have to realize that we tried with our Goetheanum to find the kind of artistic style appropriate for the new spirituality, one that would have a stimulating effect, and that with the Goetheanum that style is now, at least for the time being, completely gone. We need only express this realization to feel the tremendous pain the loss of the Goetheanum has brought.

Usually when tragedy strikes, one's opponents stop being disrespectful and scornful. However, after the tragedy of the burning of the Goetheanum our opponents think it justified and proper to oppose us with even more scorn and derision. That is indeed peculiar, and it fits in appropriately—though it is of course inappropriate—with so many other things.

The anthroposophical movement began as a purely positive activity. We did not attack anybody nor did we agitate; we just talked about the results of anthroposophical research. We calmly waited until the souls that are present on earth in our time would come to us out of their own inner impulses in order to understand what was to be conveyed out of the spiritual world. Our anthroposophical work was aimed not at wildly agitating nor at drawing up programs, but at simply telling how things are according to our researches in the spiritual world. We were waiting to see which souls had a yearning for knowledge of reality.

Many people nowadays are against anthroposophy without knowing why; they simply follow the lead of others. However, there are also a few people who know very well why they are against anthroposophy. They realize that anthroposophy reveals truths that require the jolt I described earlier—and that is something they do not want. There are many reasons why they do not want it. For example, such

135

truths used to be restricted to certain small circles. The possession of these truths then allowed people in those circles to stand above humanity as a kind of small spiritual and aristocratic elite. That is why such people hate especially those who bring the truth the spirit of the times requires out of the spiritual world and make it available to everyone. At the same time, our opponents—I am talking about the leading ones—know that nothing can be done against the truth itself. They know it will find its way through even the narrowest crevices regardless of the obstacles it might meet.

Therefore, our opponents do not usually try to fight these truths head on, for they know the latter would undoubtedly triumph. Just look at our opponents—and it would be a good thing if we anthroposophists looked at them much more often—they refrain from fighting truths openly by focusing mainly on personal attacks, insinuations, insults, and slander. They figure they cannot do anything against the truth, but nevertheless they want to do away with it. They think they can do this through personal disparagement. Their method of fighting us shows that our leading opponents know very well how to go about achieving a temporary victory.

This is what anthroposophists need to know; for many anthroposophists still believe that they can accomplish something by simply discussing things with our opponents. Nothing can harm us more than to succeed in getting our truths across in discussions, for we are not hated for telling falsehoods but for telling the truth. In fact, the more we succeed in proving we tell the truth, the more we will be hated.

Of course, this cannot stop us from standing up for the truth. But it can keep us from holding on to the naive belief that we will accomplish anything through discussions. The only thing that will help us make headway is positive work. We will make headway if we keep standing up for the truth as forcefully as we can, so that as many predestined souls as possible—there are many more in our time than one usually thinks—find their way to us and find here the spiritual nourishment they need if something constructive is to be done for the future evolution of humanity, if our future is to be an upward development rather than a regression.

It is not possible to find a way out of the chaos of our time through materialist methods. The only way to overcome the chaos of our time is the spiritual way. However, we can enter on this spiritual path only if we choose the spirit as our leader and guide. Indeed, what anthroposophists must realize and understand in the most profound sense is how to choose the spirit as their leader in the right way.

NOTES

Lecture One

1 This so-called French Course has been preserved in the following two books: Rudolf Steiner, *Philosophy, Cosmology and Religion*, vol. 215 in the Collected Works (Spring Valley, NY: Anthroposophic Press, 1984) and *Cosmology, Religion and Philosophy*, vol. 25 in the Collected Works (New York: Anthroposophic Press, 1943). The latter contains summaries of the lectures contained in the former. Rudolf Steiner prepared these summaries for the French translator of his lectures.

2 Rudolf Steiner, *The Philosophy of Freedom: A Philosophy of Spiritual Activity*, vol. 4 in the Collected Works (London: Rudolf Steiner Press, 1988).

Lecture Two

1 Karl Rosenkranz, 1805–1879, German professor of philosophy. Student of Hegel. See his book *Aus einem Tagebuch* ("From a Diary"), Leipzig, 1854, p. 328ff.

2 Georg Wilhelm Friedrich Hegel, 1770–1831. German philosopher. Last of the great German Idealist system-building philosophers; created monistic system reconciling opposites by means of dialectic process. Viewed history as similar process, dialectic of thesis and its implied antithesis leading to synthesis. Exerted great influence on Kierkegaard and Existentialists, on Marx, and on the Positivists.

Immanuel Kant, 1724–1804, German philosopher. Developed his own critical philosophy in which he sought to determine the nature and kinds of human knowledge, the necessary categories of consciousness, and their ethical and aesthetic consequences. Among other things he wrote *Critique of Pure Reason*, 1781, revised 1787.

3 No information on Bon could be found.

4 Gotthilf Heinrich von Schubert, 1780–1860, professor of natural sciences. Wrote *Symbolik des Traums ("Symbolism of Dreams")*, *1814.*

5 Johann Georg Gichtel, 1638–1710, German theosophist. Developed a mystical theology that alienated him from orthodox Lutheran doctrine. He was a disciple of Jakob Böhme and compiled the first complete edition of Böhme's works (1682–83); founded a sect that survived in Holland and Germany until recent times; synthesized his doctrine in *Theosophia practica* (1701–22).

6 Jakob Böhme, 1575–1624. German mystic. He was first a shoemaker, then had mystical experience in 1600.

7 See Lecture One, note 2.

8 Nicolaus Copernicus, 1473–1543, Polish astronomer. Made astronomical observations of orbits of sun, moon, planets. Gradually abandoned accepted Ptolemaic system of astronomy and worked out heliocentric system in which the earth rotates daily on its axis and, with other planets, revolves around the sun.

9 Rudolf Steiner, *An Outline of Occult Science*, 3rd ed., repr., (Spring Valley, NY: Anthroposophic Press, 1989). These planet names do not refer to present-day planets but to ancient evolutionary stages and are therefore capitalized.

10 Gustav Freytag, 1816–1895, German writer. Champion of German liberalism and German middle classes.
Charles John Huffam Dickens, 1812–1870, English novelist. Chief works include *Oliver Twist* (1837–39), *A Christmas Carol* (1843), *David Copperfield* (1849–50), *Bleak House* (1852–53).

Ralph Waldo Emerson, 1803–1882, American essayist, poet, and Unitarian minister. His first published work, *Nature* (1836), contained the gist of his Transcendental philosophy, which combined strains of European Romanticism, Oriental supernaturalism, and American optimism and practicality.

Lecture Three

1 Nicholas of Cusa, 1401–1464, German prelate and philosopher. Ordained, later created cardinal and bishop. Wrote treatises for church councils as well as on mathematics and philosophy. Anticipated Copernicus by his belief in the earth's rotation and revolution around the sun; conducted botanical experiments.

2 Rudolf Steiner, *Knowledge of the Higher Worlds and Its Attainment*, 3rd ed., (Hudson, NY: Anthroposophic Press, 1986).

3 Rudolf Steiner, *Von Seelenrätseln* ("Riddles of the Soul"), vol. 21 in the Collected Works (Dornach, Switzerland: Rudolf Steiner Verlag, 1983).

4 See Lecture Two, note 9.

Lecture Four

1 See Lecture Two, note 8.

2 Johann Wolfgang von Goethe, 1749–1832, leading German poet and playwright. Also wrote extensively on botany, optics, and other scientific topics.

3 *Faust* (1808–32), a drama in verse, is Goethe's masterpiece.

4 *Faust*, Part I, Night, lines 501–09. Trsl. by Stuart Atkins (Cambridge, MA: Suhrkamp/Insel Publishers Boston, 1984). All quotations from *Faust* in this volume are taken from this translation.

5 *Faust*, Part I, Martha's Garden, lines 3438–39 and 3456–57.

6 *Faust*, Prologue in Heaven, lines 243–44.

7 This is Steiner's paraphrase of Faust's lines in *Faust*, Part I, Night, lines 449–50.

8 Michel de Nostradame, or Nostradamus, 1503–1566, French physician and astrologer. Published book of rhymed prophecies under the title *Centuries* (1555). Some of his prophecies were correct.

9 See Lecture Two, note 9.

10 These names do not refer to present-day planets but to ancient evolutionary stages and are therefore capitalized.

11 Ernst Heinrich Philipp August Haeckel, 1834–1919, German biologist and philosopher. First German advocate of Darwin's theory of evolution; formulated dictum "ontogeny recapitulates phylogeny"; proposed that all nature is a unity, with life originating in crystals and evolving into the human species.

Lecture Five

1 See Lecture One, note 2.

2 Albert Einstein, 1879–1955, German-born American physicist. Developed theory of relativity, publishing account of special theory of relativity (1905) and of general theory (1916); discovered and formulated equivalence of mass and energy. Awarded 1921 Nobel prize for physics.

3 Wilhelm Conrad Röntgen, 1845–1923, German physicist. Discovered X rays (1895) and was awarded first Nobel prize for physics for this discovery (1901).

4 Novalis, pseudonym of Friedrich Leopold Freiherr von Hardenberg, 1772–1801, German poet. A leader of early Romanticists in Germany.

5 Friedrich Theodor Vischer, 1807–1887, German writer and critic. On *Faust*, see his parody, *Faust. Der Tragödie dritter Teil. Eine Parodie* ("Faust, the Third Part of the Tragedy: a Parody"), 1862.

Lecture Six

1 In connection with this lecture of February 11, 1923, Steiner made the following entries in his notebook:

The ether becomes similar to that of the nerve-sense system: A
The ether becomes similar to that of the metabolic system: B
Pus = organic matter (etheric) permeated by centrifugal astrality from the outside—on its way to the outside.

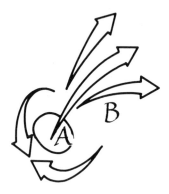

Congealed exudation = organic (etheric) matter permeated by centripetal astrality from the inside—in the process of disappearing from the physical world.

In the healing process, the organism merely continues a process that takes place everyday when poisonous outer processes invading us are fought off.

It is the *lower* system (that carries out this process); it excretes the elements [processes] from the outside after having permeated them with centrifugal forces, such as are active in the growth of plants—and in *sleep*.

The poisonous processes, however, work centripetally—in the nervous system—and bring the outer world inside after it has

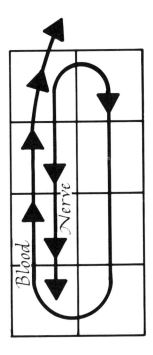

cooled it down (made it into a mere form) so that through it the spiritual can penetrate directly to the inside.

Impeded inhalation, eating, the overly forceful day processes; overly forceful exhalation, digestion, the overly forceful night processes.

The body has not taken in the spirit, the night processes are too strong = the person runs a temperature: areas of the organism soften and fester.

143

The body takes in the spirit too strongly, the day processes are too strong = the person gets cold: areas of the organism harden. Internal exudations—crumbling.

Lecture Seven

1 Friedrich Wilhelm Nietzsche, 1844–1900, German philosopher and poet. He was at first a friend and follower and later (from c.1878) a strong opponent of Wagner in art and philosophy. Opponent of Schopenhauer's philosophy; suffered mental breakdown. Known for denouncing religion, for espousing doctrine of perfectibility of human beings through forcible self-assertion, and for glorification of the superman or overman (*Übermensch*).

2 Arthur Schopenhauer, 1788–1860, German philosopher. Chief expounder of pessimism and of the irrational impulses of life arising from the will.

3 Richard Wagner, 1813–1883, German composer. Originator of the music drama and pioneer in the development of the leitmotif. Among other works, composed cycle of musical dramas based on the Siegfried saga, called collectively *Der Ring des Nibelungen*.

4 Friedrich Nietzsche, *The Birth of Tragedy and the Genealogy of Morals*, trsl. Francis Golffing, (New York: Doubleday, 1956).

5 Friedrich Nietzsche, "David Strauss the Confessor and Writer," "On the Uses and Disadvantages of History for Life," "Schopenhauer as Educator," and "Richard Wagner in Bayreuth," all in *Untimely Meditations*, trsl. R. J. Hollingsdale (Cambridge: Cambridge University Press, 1983).

6 David Friedrich Strauss, 1808–1874, German theologian and philosopher. Developed a theory of biblical interpretation based on Hegelian dialectical philosophy; caused storm of controversy among German Protestants by describing the Gospels as "historical myth." Wrote *Der alte und der neue Glaube* ("The Old and the New Faith" (1872).

7 See Friedrich Nietzsche, *Gay Science*, trsl. Walter Kaufman (New York: Vintage Books, 1974).

8 Voltaire, assumed name of François-Marie Arouet, 1694–1778. French writer. Got into trouble because of his expert satire. Gained fame as defender of victims of religious intolerance and as master of satire.

9 See Friedrich Nietzsche, *Thus Spoke Zarathustra*, trsl. R. J. Hollingsdale (Middlesex, Engl.: Penguin, 1961).

10 See Friedrich Nietzsche, *The Birth of Tragedy and the Genealogy of Morals*, trsl. Francis Golffing, (New York: Doubleday, 1956).

11 Friedrich Nietzsche, *Beyond Good and Evil*, trsl. Walter Kaufman (New York: Vintage Books, 1966).

Lecture Eight

1 Johann Friedrich Herbart, 1776–1841, German philosopher and educator. Developed a general metaphysical theory of pluralistic realism, important especially for its psychology, which rejected notions of faculties and innate ideas and constructed full theory on which to ground a pedagogy similar to that of Pestalozzi.

2 See Lecture Seven, note 11.

Lecture Nine

1 John Scotus Erigena, c. 810–877, Irish-born theologian and philosopher. Wrote *De divisione naturae* (862–866), his major work, in which he attempted to reconcile Neoplatonist emanationism and Christian creationism. His doctrine was long influential, especially in its mystical implications, but was ultimately condemned because of its pantheistic leaning.

2 Johann Christoph Friedrich von Schiller, 1759–1805, German poet, playwright, and critic. Wrote *Letters on the Aesthetic Education of Man* (1795). See also Lecture Four, note 2.

3 Paul Deussen, 1845–1919, German philosopher and Sanskrit scholar.

4 Rudolf Steiner, *Goethe's Conception of the World*, vol. 6 in the Collected Works (New York: Anthroposophic Press, 1928).

5 Friedrich Nietzsche, *Die Philosophie im tragischen Zeitalter der Griechen* ("Philosophy in the Tragic Age of the Greeks"), 1873.

6 Thales of Miletus, c.625–c.547 B.C. Greek philosopher and scientist. One of the Seven Wise Men of Greece. He taught that water, or moisture, was the one element from which the world was formed.

Heraclitus, c.540–c.480 B.C. Greek philosopher. Evolved cosmology in which fire is the principal element, all things are in a state of dynamic equilibrium, apparent opposites are actually bound by underlying connection, and the whole is a manifestation of logos. Later interpreted by Plato to have claimed all things are in constant flux. Writings extant only in fragments notable for their difficulty.

Anaxagoras, c.500–c.428 B.C. Greek philosopher. First to introduce dualistic explanation of universe; held that all natural objects are composed of infinitesimally small particles containing mixtures of all qualities, and that mind or intelligence (*nous*) acts upon masses of these particles to produce objects.

7 Parmenides, born c.515 B.C. Greek philosopher of Elea. Only fragments of his work are extant. One of Plato's dialogues was named after him.

8 See Lecture One, note 2.

Publisher's Note

The lectures printed here were given by Rudolf Steiner to audiences familiar with the general background and terminology of his anthroposophical teaching. It should be remembered that in his autobiography *The Course of My Life*, he emphasizes the distinction between his written works on the one hand, and on the other, reports of lectures that were given as oral communications and were not originally intended for print. For an intelligent appreciation of the lectures it should be borne in mind that certain premises were taken for granted when the words were spoken. "These premises," Rudolf Steiner writes, "include at the very least the anthroposophical knowledge of Man and of the Cosmos in its spiritual essence; also what may be called 'anthroposophical history,' told as an outcome of research into the spiritual world."

28·29·30·31